Out of Joint and Sydney Theatre Company present

THE CONVICT'S OPERA

by Stephen Jeffreys

adapted from *The Beggar's Opera* by John Gay

First performed 30 September 2008 at Sydney Theatre.
First UK performance 15 January 2009 at Salisbury Playhouse.

out of joint

Our Country's Good
(Photo: John Haynes)

"You expect something special from Out of Joint"
The Times

Out of Joint is a national and international touring theatre company dedicated to the development and production of new writing. Under the direction of Max Stafford-Clark the company has premiered plays from leading writers including David Hare, Caryl Churchill, David Edgar, Alistair Beaton, Sebastian Barry and Timberlake Wertenbaker, as well as introducing first-time writers such as Simon Bennett, Stella Feehily and Mark Ravenhill.

"Max Stafford-Clark's excellent Out of Joint company"
The Independent

Flight Path
(Photo: Graham Michael)

Touring all over the UK, Out of Joint frequently performs at and co-produces with key venues such as the Royal Court and the National Theatre. The company has performed in six continents – most recently a world tour of its Africa-inspired *Macbeth*. Back home, Out of Joint also pursues an extensive education programme.

"Out of Joint is out of this world"
Boston Globe

Out of Joint's other productions for 2009 include *Dreams of Violence* by Stella Feehily (with Soho Theatre) and *Mixed Up North* by Robin Soans.

Director: **Max Stafford-Clark**
Producer: **Graham Cowley**
Marketing Manager: **Jon Bradfield**
Administrator & Education Manager:
Maeve McKeown
Assistant Director: **Clare Lizzimore**
Literary Manager: **Alex Yates**
Finance Officer: **Sandra Palumbo**

Board of Directors Kate Ashfield, Linda Bassett, John Blackmore (Chair), Elyse Dodgson, Sonia Friedman, Stephen Jeffreys, Paul Jesson, Danny Sapani, Karl Sydow

Out of Joint
7 Thane Works, Thane Villas, London N7 7NU
Tel: 020 7609 0207   Fax: 020 7609 0203
Email: ojo@outofjoint.co.uk
Web: www.outofjoint.co.uk

Macbeth
(Photo: John Haynes)

KEEP IN TOUCH
For information on our shows, tour details and offers, get in touch (contact details above) letting us know whether you'd like to receive information by post or email.

BOOKSHOP
Scripts of many of our previous shows are available at exclusive discounted prices from our online shop:
www.outofjoint.co.uk

EDUCATION
Out of Joint offers a diverse programme of workshops and discussions for groups coming to see our performances. For full details of our education programme, resource packs or Our Country's Good workshops, contact Maeve at Out of Joint.

Shopping and Fucking
(Photo: John Haynes)

Out of Joint is grateful to the following for their support over the years: Arts Council England, The Foundation for Sport and the Arts, The Baring Foundation, The Paul Hamlyn Foundation, The Olivier Foundation, The Peggy Ramsay Foundation, The John S Cohen Foundation, The David Cohen Charitable Trust, The National Lottery through the Arts Council of England, The Prudential Awards, Stephen Evans, Karl Sydow, Harold Stokes and Friends of Theatre, John Lewis Partnership, Royal Victoria Hall Foundation. Out of Joint is a Registered Charity No. 1033059

Principal Sponsor

The Wharf

Led by Artistic Directors, Cate Blanchett and Andrew Upton, Sydney Theatre Company (STC) is the premier theatre company in Australia and has been a major force in Australian drama since its establishment in 1978. The Company presents an annual twelve-play program at its home on Sydney Harbour, The Wharf; at the nearby Sydney Theatre; and at the Drama Theatre as the resident theatre company of the Sydney Opera House.

STC offers Sydney audiences an eclectic program of Australian plays, lively interpretations of the classic repertoire and the best of new international writing. It also produces a significant Education program for schools and, in its studio space, produces work created by emerging playwrights and theatre-makers, originating in 1988 with Baz Lurhmann's Six Years Old company and, in its current identity, as Next Stage. The Company reaches outside Sydney, touring productions throughout Australia and internationally and plays annually to total audiences in excess of 300,000.

STC has launched and fostered the theatre careers of many of Australia's internationally renowned artists including Mel Gibson, Judy Davis, Hugo Weaving, Miranda Otto, Geoffrey Rush, Toni Collette, Rose Byrne and Cate Blanchett.

STC actively fosters relationships and collaborations with international artists and companies. Renowned directors Michael Blakemore, Max Stafford-Clark, Howard Davies, Declan Donnellan and Philip Seymour Hoffman have worked with STC in recent years, and the company has presented productions by Complicite, Cheek by Jowl, Out of Joint and the National Theatre of Great Britain.

In 2001 STC performed at the Brooklyn Academy of Music in New York with its production of The White Devil and returned in 2006 with its production of Hedda Gabler. STC will again feature at BAM later this year with a new production of A Streetcar Named Desire, to be directed by Liv Ullman, which will also tour to the Kennedy Centre in Washington. In 2002 the STC production of The Cherry Pickers enjoyed an extensive tour of the UK which included seasons at the Cultureshock Festival in Manchester and at the prestigious Brighton and Salisbury Festivals.

Sydney Theatre

sydneytheatre.com.au

Sydney Theatre Company
Pier 4, Hickson Road,
Walsh Bay NSW 2000
PO Box 777, Millers Point NSW 2000

Patron:
Mr Giorgio Armani

Australian Government
Department of Foreign Affairs and Trade

Australian Government

Australia | Council
for the Arts

This project is supported by the Australian Government
through the Australia Council for the Arts and the
Australia International Cultural Council, in initiative of the
Department of Foreign Affairs and Trade.

UK TOUR 2009

15 – 24 January
Salisbury Playhouse
01722 320333
www.salisburyplayhouse.com

27 – 31 January
Everyman Theatre, Cheltenham
01242 572 573
www.everymantheatre.org.uk

3 – 7 February
Library Theatre, Manchester
0161 236 7110
www.librarytheatre.com

10 – 14 February
Oxford Playhouse
01865 305305
www.oxfordplayhouse.com

17 – 21 February
Nuffield Theatre, Southampton
023 8067 1771
www.nuffieldtheatre.co.uk

24 – 28 February
West Yorkshire Playhouse, Leeds
0113 213 7700
www.wyplayhouse.com

3 – 7 March
Warwick Arts Centre
024 7652 4524
www.warwickartscentre.co.uk

10 – 14 March
Liverpool Playhouse
0151 709 4776
www.everymanplayhouse.com

THE COMPANY

Lucy Lockit/Amelia Whiting/Dolly Trull	Amelia Cormack
Lockit/Eddie Cosgrove	Peter Cousens
John Gay/William/Matt of Mint/Mrs Vixen	Glenn Butcher
Filch/Tom Jenner	Thomas Eyre
Diana Trapes/Phebe	Karina Fernandez
Captain MacNaughton/Bartlemy/Ben Budge	Nicholas Goode
MacHeath/Harry Morton	Juan Jackson
Polly Peachum/Grace Madden	Ali McGregor
Peachum/Ben Barnwell	Brian Protheroe
Mrs Peachum/Bett Rock	Catherine Russell

Director	Max Stafford-Clark
Musical Director	Felix Cross
Choreographer	John O'Connell
Set Designer	Dale Ferguson
Costume Designer	Tess Schofield
Lighting Designer	Nick Schlieper
Sound Designer	Paul Charlier
Assistant Director	Iain Sinclair
Assistant Director (UK)	Clare Lizzimore
Assistant to the Director	Stella Feehily
Voice and Text Coach	Charmian Gradwell

Production Manager (Sydney)	Annie Eves-Boland
Production Manager	Gary Beestone *for Giraffe*
Tour Production Manager	Spencer New *for Giraffe*
Company and Stage Manager	Richard Llewelyn
Deputy Stage Manager	Sarah Smith
Associate Lighting Designer	Tim Bray
Associate Sound Designer	Helen Atkinson
Wardrobe Supervisor	Ara Moradian

Rehearsal photography by Olivia Martin-McGuire

COMPANY BIOGRAPHIES

GLENN BUTCHER
William/Matt of Mint/
John Gay/Mrs Vixen
Glenn's **theatre** includes
Dusty - The Musical; *Singing
in the Rain*; *Venetian Twins*
(Olympic Arts Festival);
Chicago; *The New Rocky
Horror Show*; *Follies Concert*
(Sydney Opera House); *The
Headbutt* (Belvoir Street
Theatre). **Comedy** includes
The Melbourne International
Comedy Festival and The
Castanet Club. **TV** includes
Monster House, *Kath and
Kim*, *Playschool*, *Full Frontal*,
Fast Forward, *The Big Gig*, *A
Country Practice*, *Swap Shop*,
The Money or The Gun. **Film:**
Young Einstein, *Pizza: The
Movie*, *Soft Fruit*, *The Castanet
Club*.

PAUL CHARLIER
Sound Designer
For Sydney Theatre Company
(as composer): *The Serpent's
Teeth*, *Love-Lies-Bleeding*,
Troupers, *Woman in Mind*,
The Cherry Orchard, *Influence*,
Scenes from a Separation, *The
Miser*, *Victory*, *Amigos*, *The
Way of the World*, *Soulmates*,
The Floating World, *Heartbreak
House*; as Sound Designer:
Hedda Gabler (New York
Season), *Democracy*, *The
Real Thing*, *The Breath Of*

Life, *Copenhagen*, *Three
Days of Rain*, *A Cheery
Soul* (co-production with
Company B). Other work
as a composer for **theatre**:
Afterlife (National Theatre,
UK); *Honour Bound* (Sydney
Opera House/Malthouse);
Already Elsewhere (Force
Majeure); *Toy Symphony*,
The Lieutenant of Inishmore,
Buried Child, *Suddenly Last
Summer*, *The Seagull*, *WASP*,
A View From The Bridge,
The Blind Giant is Dancing,
Aftershocks (Company B);
The Cost of Living/Can We
Afford This (DV8 Physical
Theatre); *Ruby's Last Dollar*,
Last Cab to Darwin (Porkchop
Productions); *Live Acts on
Stage* (Black Swan); *The Fire
on the Snow*, *The Shifting
Heart*, *A Little Like Drowning*
(STCSA): *Eclipse*, *Possessed/
Dispossessed* (Entr'Acte
Theatre); *Blood Vessel* (Stalker
Theatre); *Presence*, *Chilling
and Killing my Annabel Lee*,
Slippery When Wet (Griffin).
Film: *Candy*; *The Cost of
Living*, *Green Eyes*, *Friends and
Enemies* (DV8). **TV:** *Aftershocks*
(ABC TV), *One Australia* (SBS
TV). Other work as Sound
Designer, for **theatre**: *Deuce*
(Music Box Theatre, New
York); *The Underpants*, *Waiting
For Godot*, *My Zinc Bed*, *The
Little Cherry Orchard*, *As You
Like It*, *The Judas Kiss*, *The
Alchemist*, *Night on Bald
Mountain*, *The Governor's
Family*, *Hamlet*, *Radiance*, *A
Little Like Drowning* (Company
B); *Incognita* (Stalker). **Film:**
Looking for Alibrandi, *The
Projectionist*. **Installations:**
Further Faster Higher
(Powerhouse Museum); *Those
Final Moments*, *Proxy*. **Radio:**
A Plan For Eurydice (ABC), *The
Touring Machine* (MoCA, LA),
*The Last Chances of Johnny
Zhivago* (BAM Next Wave), *Iwo
Jima Souvenir*, *Remembrance
Day*. **Awards:** Sydney

Theatre and Greenroom
Awards for the Score of
Honour Bound.

AMELIA CORMACK
Lucy Lockit/Amelia Whiting/
Dolly Trull
Amelia trained in Musical
Theatre at WAAPA. **Theatre**
includes *Joseph and the
Amazing Technicolour
Dreamcoat*; *United States of
Nothing* (Griffin Stablemates);
The Hatpin, *Up Close and
Musical* (Kookaburra); *Priscilla
Queen of the Desert – the
Musical*. **Cabaret** includes
Shopping Centre Santa and
Love for Sale. **Film** includes
Gone. **TV** includes: *The Silence*
and *All Saints*. Awards: 2008
Green Room Award for
Best Featured Ensemble for
Priscilla, Queen of the Desert.

PETER COUSENS
Lockit/Eddie Cosgrove
Peter's previous work with
Sydney Theatre Company

includes *Hamlet, Chicago, Chinchilla, Nicholas Nickebly, Measure for Measure* and *Macbeth*. Other **theatre** includes *Company* (MTC); *You Never Can Tell, Breaker Morant, The Sentimental Bloke, Camille* (QTC); *The Falls* (Griffin). Musical theatre includes *Showboat; West Side Story; Blood Brothers; The Hatpin; Camelot; The Phantom of the Opera* (West End and in Australia); *Miss Saigon; Les Miserables; Aspects of Love; The Mikado; Fiddler on the Roof* (Opera Australia); *Sweeney Todd, Boojum* (Opera SA). **Recordings** include *Corner of the Sky, From a Distance, A Life On Earth, Miss Saigon International Symphonic*. Peter's career has evolved with his creation of Kookaburra: The National Music Theatre Company, aiming to be a leading producer, developer and advocate of musical theatre in Australia. Peter has produced *Pippin, Company, Up Close and Musical, An Audience With Stephen Sondheim* and this year will produce *Tell Me On A Sunday* and *Little Women* for Kookaburra. Peter appears by kind permission of the board of Kookaburra.

FELIX CROSS
Musical Director

Felix's previous work for Out of Joint includes *Macbeth, Talking to Terrorists, O Go My Man* and *The Overwhelming*. He is Artistic Director of Nitro, Britain's black music theatre company, where his work includes *The Wedding Dance* (writer and co-director), *Mass Carib* (composer and director), *Slamdunk* (writer and co-director) *Passports to the Promised Land* (writer and composer), *Up Against the Wall* (writer), *Tricksters Payback* (composer), *Iced*

(director), *An African Cargo* (director), *An Evening of Soul Food* (director). Other **theatre** includes *Ghostdancing, Ryman & The Sheik, Strictly Dandia, A Fine Balance* (Tamasha); *The Bottle Imp, Jekyll & Hyde* (Major Road); *Blues For Railton, Mass Carib, King Lear* (Albany Empire). Felix has also worked for Nottingham Playhouse, Chichester Festival Theatre, Tricycle, The Nottingham Gate Theatre, Southwalk Playhouse, Hampstead Theatre and the Greenwich Theatre.

THOMAS EYRE
Filch/Tom Jenner

Thomas recently graduated from Bristol Old Vic Theatre School, where he performed in another *Beggar's Opera* reworking: *The Threepenny Opera*, as well as a lead role in the brand new Musical Revue *Crackers & Spice*. Other **theatre** includes *Spiders* (Soho Theatre) and *Single Spies* (No 1 UK Tour).

DALE FERGUSON
Set Designer

Designs for Sydney Theatre Company include: *Don's Party, The 25th Putnam County Spelling Bee, Summer Rain, Howard Katz, Great Expectations, A Cheery Soul, The Girl Who Saw Everything, Sylvia, Nightfall, Trelawny of the Wells. The Shaughraun.*

Other **theatre**: *Antigone, Exit the King, Peribanez, The Chairs, The Sapphires, The Judas Kiss, The Marriage of Figaro, The Dreamers, The Aunt's Story* (Company B); *The Rocky Horror Show; Titanic – The Musical* (Seabiscuit); *The History Boys, The Glass Soldier, Don's Party, Female of the Species, The Glass Menagerie, Memory of Water, The Seagull, Design for Living, The Chairs, The Resistible Rise of Arturo Ui, Amy's View, True West* (MTC); *Woman-Bomb, Exit the King* (Malthouse Theatre). **Opera** includes, for Welsh National Opera: *Aridane Auf Naxos* and *The Marriage of Figaro* (co-production with Opera Australia); *The Children's Bach, Motherland, Fresh Ghosts* (Chamber Made Opera). **TV:** 2008 Logie Awards, *The Price is Right, Temptation*. Dale was Resident Designer for Queensland Theatre Company 1990-1994 and at Melbourne Theatre Company 1995-1998. **Awards:** Green Room Awards for Best Design for *The Seagull, Cheery Soul, Dealers Choice, Molly Sweeney*; Loudon Sainthill Travelling Scholarship.

STELLA FEEHILY
Assistant to the Director

Stella is a playwright whose work for Out of Joint and the Royal Court includes *Think global, f**k local* (Royal Court "Rough Cuts"), *O Go My Man* and *Duck*. Other writing includes *Catch* (writing collaboration for the Royal Court); *GAME, Sweet Bitter* (Fishamble). As Assistant: *The Overwhelming* for the Roundabout Theatre, New York; and *Mixed Up North* (LAMDA).

KARINA FERNANDEZ
Diana Trapes/Phebe
Karina previously appeared with Out of Joint in *Blue Heart* and *Shopping and F***king*. Other theatre includes *Trips* (Birmingham Rep); *Cool Water Murder* (Belgrade Theatre, Coventry); *Romeo and Juliet* (UK tour); *Dealing with Claire* (Union Theatre); *Passion* (Chelsea Theatre); *Cahoot's Macbeth* (King's Head); *Hamlet* (Globe Theatre, Neuss); *Bites* (Bush); *Woody Allen's Murder Mysteries* (Croydon Warehouse); *Crocodile Seeking Refuge, The Boy Who Left Home* (Lyric Hammersmith); *Mrs Pat* (Theatre Royal, York); *Macbeth* (Bristol Old Vic); *Wedding Day at the Cro-Magnons* (Soho). **Films** include: *Happy Go Lucky, The Return, Gabriel*. **TV** includes: *The Forsythe Saga, Happy Birthday Shakespeare*.

NICHOLAS GOODE
**Captain MacNaughton/
Bartlemy/Ben Budge/
Musician**
Theatre includes *Tom's Midnight Garde*n (Nottingham Playhouse); *Around the World in 80 Days, Under the Blue Sky, Rebecca* (Theatre by the Lake, Keswick); *A Christmas Carol, A Child's Christmas in Wales* (Wales Theatre Company); *Fiddler on the Roof* (Aberystwyth Arts Centre); *In One Ear* (Lyric Studio); *Fear and Misery in the Third Reich* (Watford Palace); *The Tempest* (Oddsocks); *The Settlement* (BAC); *Oliver Twist* (Lyric Hammersmith). *The Damask Drum* (Greenwich Playhouse); *A Real Princess* (Blue Elephant).

CHARMIAN GRADWELL
Voice and Text Coach
Charmian is the STC voice and text coach where work includes *Romeo and Juliet* (Education) and *Gallipoli*. As a voice coach, other **theatre** includes *Julius Caesar, The Tempest, The Canterbury Tales, A Winter's Tale, Pericles, Days of Significance, Macbeth, Macbett, The Penelopiad, Noughts and Crosses,* 'The Comedies' London Season, *A Midsummer Night's Dream*. As Director, Deviser and Trainer: 1999 season at Space 2000 in Kaduna, Nigeria; The London Shakespeare Workout (Shakespeare in prisons). As Movement Director: *Comedy of Errors, A Chorus of Disapproval, Winter's Tale*. Charmian's acting career has encompassed the West End, musicals, touring, repertory, TV and radio. She has coached voice and dialects for a variety of theatre and television companies in the UK and was the voice trainer for the London School of Puppetry. She has led voice workshops and master classes in Europe, North America and Asia. Charmian also represented Great Britain in marathon kayak racing, winning gold at the World Masters in 1997.

JUAN JACKSON
MacHeath/Harry Morton
Juan appeared in *Sweet Bird of Youth* for Melbourne Theatre Company. **Musicals** include *Miss Saigon; Man of La Mancha; Cats; West Side Story* (Orlando Civic Theatre); *Hair*. **Opera** appearances include: *From The Lip, Teorema* (Chamber Made Opera); *The Merry Widow, Bach – Lieberieder Waltzes* (Opera Australia); *Porgy and Bess* (Houston Grand Opera/Living Arts); *Chanticleer, The Music Shop* (South Georgia Opera). **Concert** appearances include *Concert of American Music Theatre* with the Australian Pops Orchestra and *Barber*

to Bernstein with Sydney Symphony Orchestra at Sydney Festival. **Recordings** include *Old American Songs* for ABC Classics.

STEPHEN JEFFREYS
Writer
The Convict's Opera is Stephen's fourth successive play to be premiered outside his native England, following last year's *The Art of War* at Sydney Theatre Company (directed by his wife Annabel Arden), *Lost Land* at Steppenwolf, Chicago (starring John Malkovich) and *Interruptions* at UC Davis, California. Stephen is perhaps best known for his play about the Earl of Rochester *The Libertine* which was premiered by Out of Joint at the Royal Court, London in 1995 and received its US premiere at Steppenwolf Theatre, Chicago in 1996 with John Malkovich in the leading role. The film of *The Libertine*, starring Johnny Depp, for which Stephen wrote the screenplay, was released in 2005. *I Just Stopped by to see the Man* received an AT&T Plays On Stage award, again premiering at the Royal Court and Steppenwolf. His other plays include *Valued Friends* (Evening Standard Most Promising Playwright Award 1989), *A Going Concern, The Clink* and *Like Dolls and Angels* (National Student Drama Festival 1977). His adaptation of Dickens' *Hard Times* has received many productions in the US and his version of Richard Brome's *A Jovial Crew*, directed by Max Stafford-Clark, was a hit for the Royal Shakespeare Company in 1992. Stephen was Literary Associate of the Royal Court for eleven years. He is a much sought after teacher of playwriting and film script

doctor. He has just finished a screenplay about Florence Nightingale for Ecosse.

ALI MCGREGOR
Polly Peachum/
Grace Madden
Ali trained at the Royal Northern College of Music in Manchester. **Opera** credits include *The Magic Flute, La Cenerentola, Iolanthe, Don Giovanni, Fidelio, Sweeney Todd, L'Elisir d'Amore, The Mikado, Manon, Il Combattimento di Tancredi e Clorinda, The Love for Three Oranges, Trial By Jury, Die Fledermaus* (Opera Australia); *Il Pomo d'Oro* (Batignano Opera Festival, Italy); *The Spirit of Vienna, Il Tabarro, Jacques Brel is Alive and Well and Living in Paris* (Clonter Opera, UK); *The Silverlake, The Beggar's Opera* (Broomhill Opera at Wilton's Music Hall); *Don Giovanni* (New Zealand Opera). She performed with Sydney Symphony Orchestra in *Barber to Bernstein*. Cabaret includes *La Clique – a Sideshow Burlesque*, and *The Opera Burlesque*, in the Famous Spiegeltent (Melbourne, Adelaide and Edinburgh Fringe Festivals). Ali's **recordings** include the title song and soundtrack to the Australian feature film *One Perfect Day; Love of Three Oranges; Trial by Jury* (ABC DVD); and her independently

released EP *Midnight Lullabies*. **TV** includes presenting Channel 4's live telecast of *La Traviata* (Paris 2000) and regular appearances on ABC's *Spicks and Specks*.

JOHN O'CONNELL
Choreographer
Previously for Sydney Theatre Company: *Tales of the Vienna Woods*. Other **theatre** includes: *The Rocky Horror Picture Show* (New Theatricals); *Company* (Kookaburra); *The Threepenny Opera, Keating, the Musical* (Company B). *Six Dance Lessons in Six Weeks* (Ensemble); *A Midsummer Night's Dream* (Opera Australia); *Venetian Twins* (QTC); *Kissing Frogs* (Glynn Nicholas Group); Barry Humphries One Man Show: *Remember You're Out; South Pacific* (GFO); *Sweet Charity, The Pajama Game, Assassins, Kiss Me Kate* and *Once on this Island* (NIDA); *Borderline Cases* (Flying Trapeze Theatre); *Mr Cha Cha Says Dance* (Perth Festival 2005). **Film** includes: *Shall We Dance, Moulin Rouge, Strictly Ballroom, Razzle Dazzle, Romeo & Juliet, Muriel's Wedding, Peter Pan, Passion, The Quiet American, The Matrix Revolutions, Scooby Doo, Children of the Revolution, Me, Myself & I*, and most recently, *Enchanted* and Baz Luhrmann's *Australia*. **TV:** Academy Awards 2008, *Come in Spinner, Brides of Christ, The Party Machine, Lucinda Smith, Dancing Daze, Body Business, Videopix*. John has been the Staging Director for *Il Divo*. **Awards** include Best Choreography at the American Choreography Awards for *Moulin Rouge* and an Australian Dance Award for Contribution to the Art of Dance.

BRIAN PROTHEROE
Peacham/Ben Barnwell
Brian previously appeared with Out of Joint in *Three Sisters*, *Break of Day* and *Some Explicit Polaroids*. He was born in Salisbury and since 1966 he has successfully managed to combine his acting and **music** career: during the 1970's he released a number of pop records and has also composed music for a number of pantomimes at the Theatre Royal, Stratford East, London. Other **theatre** includes *Leave Him to Heaven*, the original London cast of the American musical *Pump Boys and Dinettes*, and *The Lord of the Rings* (West End); *The Birthday Party* (Bristol Old Vic); title role in *Macbeth* (Derby Playhouse); *Losing Louis* (Hampstead and West End); *The Price* (Act UK Tour); *The Cherry Orchard* (Oxford Stage Company); *The Tempest*, *The Winters Tale*, *Pericles* (RSC); and *The Sisters Rosensweig* (Old Vic). Brian has also taken part in concert performances of *A Midsummer Night's Dream* with the City of London Sinfonia. Television work includes *Midsommer Murders*, *Love Soup*, *55 Degrees North*, *Holby City*, *Heartbeat*, *Not a Penny More, Not a Penny Less*, *Leave Him to Heaven*, *Titus Andronicus*, *Henry VI* and *Richard III*. Brian has also appeared in several

television series including *Dr. Willoughby*, *The Hello Girls*, *Real Women II*, *Gentlemen and Players* and *Shrinks*. **Film** appearances include *The Biographer*, *Commedia*, *The Biggest Bank Robbery* and *Superman*.

CATHERINE RUSSELL
Mrs Peacham/Bett Rock
Catherine appeared in Out of Joint's *Talking to Terrorists*, *The Break of Day* and *Three Sisters*. Other **theatre** includes *The Day I Stood Still* (National Theatre); *After the Dance* (Oxford Stage Company); *A Chaste Maid in Cheapside*, *Venus and Lucrece* (Almeida); *The Last Carnival* (Birmingham Rep); *The Ghost Train*, *Sailor Beware* (Lyric Hammersmith). *The Waltz of Toreadors* (Chichester Festival); *The Way of the World*, *Arms and the Man* (Royal Exchange, Manchester); *Martha, Josie and the Chinese Elvis* (Salisbury Playhouse). **Film** includes: *Bridget Jones: The Edge Of Reason*, *Clockwork Mice*, *Solitaire For 2*, *Soft Top, Hard Shoulder*, *The Lake*. **TV** includes the television series *Chandler and Co*, *The Cazalets*, *Inspector Linley*, *Always and Everyone*, *Single*, *Chelworth*. Guest appearances in *Poirot*, *Messiah 3*, *Waking the Dead*, *Silent Witness*, *The Bill*, *Outside the Rules*, *The Secretary Who*

Stole 4 Million, *Eastenders*, *Sea Of Souls*, *Sherlock Holmes – The Problem at Thor Bridge*, *Airbase*, *Maigret*, *The Vision Thing*, *Wilderness*, *Holding On*, *Unsuitable Job for a Women*.

NICK SCHLIEPER
Lighting Designer
For Sydney Theatre Company: *The Serpent's Teeth*, *The Year of Magical Thinking*, *Blackbird*, *The Season at Sarsaparilla*, *A Kind of Alaska/Reunion*, *Hedda Gabler* (2006 New York season, 2004 and in 1986), *Mother Courage and Her Children*, *Victory*, *Howard Katz*, *Inheritance*, *A Doll's House*, *Volpone*, *Don Juan*, *Three Sisters*, *Cyrano de Bergerac*, *A Delicate Balance*, *The Life of Galileo*, *As You Like It*, *Pentecost*, *Les Parents Terribles*, Other **theatre**: *Ninety*, *The Glass Soldier*, *The Visit*, *Inheritance*, *Proof*, *Measure for Measure*, *The Tempest*, *Great Expectations*, *Comedy of Errors* (MTC): *The Unexpected Man*, *Lulu*, *Black Mary* (Company B): *Hamlet*, *Troilus and Cressida*, *Othello* (Bell Shakespeare); *Cosi*, *'Tis Pity She's A Whore*, *A Midsummer Night's Dream*, *Marat/Sade* (STCSA). *The Tempest*, *Good Works* (and set design) (QTC). **Opera** includes *Don Giovanni*, *Nabucco*, *Trovatore*, *Der Freischütz*, *Andrea Chenier*, *The Elixir of Love*, *The Abduction from the Seraglio*, *Tannhäuser*, *Falstaff*, Ken Russell's *Madam Butterfly*, *Don Giovanni*, *The Flying Dutchman* (Opera Australia); Wagner's *Ring Cycle* (lighting and associate set designer), *Parsifal*, *Salome* (and set design) (State Opera South Australia); and lighting and set design for *Don Giovanni* (Opera Queensland). Work outside of Australia includes *The Hostage* (RSC); *The Government Inspector* (Theatre Clwyd); *The Ginger Man*,

Armut, Reichtum (Hamburg); *Kasimir und Karoline*, Lea's *Hochzeit* (Vienna); U.F.A. Revue (Berlin and Kennedy Centre, Washington); *Michael Kramer, Ein Florentinerhut* (Schillertheater); Michael Bogdanov's *Macbeth* and *Peer Gynt* (State Theatre of Bavaria); Set and lighting for *Macbeth* (Opera NZ); *Tales of Hoffmann* (Wiesbaden); *A Midsummer Night's Dream, Billy Budd* (Hamburg Opera). Awards: Melbourne Green Room Awards for *Falstaff, The Visit* and *Boomerang*. 2004 Helpmann Award for Bangarra Dance Company's *Bush*.

TESS SCHOFIELD
Costume Designer

Previously for Sydney Theatre Company: *The Great, The Serpent's Teeth, Riflemind, A Midsummer Night's Dream, The Art of War, Woman in Mind, Mother Courage and Her Children, Far Away, Victory, Love For Love, The Government Inspector, The Trackers Of Oxyrhynchus* and *The Mortal Falcon* – Tess was Resident Designer 2007. Other **theatre**: *Toy Symphony, Snugglepot & Cuddlepie And The Adventures Of Little Ragged Blossom, A Midsummer's Night Dream, The Lieutenant Of Inishmore, Waiting for Godot, Cloudstreet, Suddenly Last Summer, As You Like It, The Judas Kiss, The Govenor's Family, The Seagull, Night On Bald Mountain, The Cockroach Opera, Diary Of a Madman, Knuckledusters, Les Enfants Du Paradis, A Lie of the Mind* (Company B); *Chess* (Theatre Royal); Caucasian Chalk Circle, Spring Awakening (ATYP). **Opera** includes *Sweeney Todd* (Lyric Opera of Chicago/Royal Opera House Covent Garden); *Jenufa, Lady Macbeth Of Mtsensk* and

Whitsunday (Opera Australia). **Film:** *Unfolding Florence, Dirty Deeds, Bootmen, Spotswood, Radiance, Cosi, Mr Reliable, Greenkeeping.*

IAIN SINCLAIR
Assistant Director

Iain's work for Sydney Theatre Company includes as Assistant Director includes *Blackbird, Troupers, Festen.* Other **theatre** (as Director): *The Seed* (Company B); *Lord of the Flies, Hurlyburly* (Stables); *The Seed, My Arm, A Streetcar Named Datsun 120Y* (B Sharp); *Beyond the Neck* (Tasmania Performs); *Harry's Christmas* (TRS); *Lounge.Room.Culture, The Fever, The Designated Mourner, How I learned to Drive, The Romans in Britain, Deviations, Hitting Town, Shopping and F***ing, Cloud 9, All My Sleep and Waking, This is our Yoth, Norm and Ahmed* (Elbow Theatre); *Shakespeare A La Carte* (Canberra Youth Theatre); *How I Learned to Drive* (Canberra Repertory). **Awards** include: 2007 Sydney Theatre Award for Best Independent Production for *The Seed*. 1998, 2000, 2001, 2002 Canberra Critics Circle Awards. Iain trained at the Royal Academy of Dramatic Art, and King's College London, Churchill Fellow, Queens Trust Scholar.

MAX STAFFORD-CLARK
Director

Educated at Trinity College, Dublin, Max Stafford-Clark co-founded Joint Stock Theatre Group in 1974 following his Artistic Directorship of The Traverse Theatre, Edinburgh. From 1979 to 1993 he was Artistic Director of The Royal Court Theatre. In 1993 he founded the touring company, Out of Joint. His work as a Director has overwhelmingly been

with new writing, and he has commissioned and directed first productions by many leading writers, including Sue Townsend, Stephen Jeffreys, Timberlake Wertenbaker, Sebastian Barry, April de Angelis, Mark Ravenhill, Andrea Dunbar, Robin Soans, Alistair Beaton, Stella Feehily, David Hare and Caryl Churchill. In addition he has directed classic texts including *The Seagull, The Recruiting Officer* and *King Lear* for the Royal Court; *A Jovial Crew, The Wives' Excuse* and *The Country Wife* for The Royal Shakespeare Company; and *The Man of Mode, She Stoops to Conquer, Three Sisters* and *Macbeth* for Out of Joint. He directed David Hare's *The Breath of Life* for Sydney Theatre Company in 2003. Academic credits include an honorary doctorate from Oxford Brookes University and Visiting Professorships at the Universities of Hertfordshire, Warwick and York. His books are *Letters to George* and *Taking Stock*.

THE CONVICT'S OPERA
Max Stafford-Clark

It's wise from the outset to make a few points about *The Convict's Opera*. It is of course only the latest in a long line of sequels that all spring from the eighteenth century's extraordinary hit. *The Threepenny Opera* is the best known but the eighteenth century alone saw *The Beggar's Wedding*, *The Beggar's Banquet* and an all-child production in Dublin dubbed *The Beggar's Brats*. They stopped short only at *The Beggar's Bar mitzvah*.

The Cambridge Companion to British Theatre, 1730–1830 makes it evident that opera itself was an evolving form during this period and it was comparatively unusual to have an opera by one composer: for example the comic opera *Tom Jones*, produced at Covent Garden in 1676, was based not on Fielding's novel but on a subsequent French adaptation. It included music drawn from a long list of composers: an overture from Piccini, a finale set to the last movement of Corelli's *Concerto Grosso in F* and tunes from Abel, Arne, Arnold, JS Bach, Baildon, Bates, Boyce, Galuppi, Granon, Handel, Holcombe, Pergoleci and Van Maldere with Old King Cole and Roger de Coverley thrown in for good measure. Gray himself borrowed tunes from Handel, Bononcini and Bach so in recruiting Leonard Cohen, Neil Young, Marvin Gay, The Pogues and The Gypsy Punks, we are simply following the path John Gay laid out.

Moreover transportation was, it turns out, very much on Gay's mind. Gay wrote a sequel to *The Beggar's Opera* called *Polly*. It was never performed because Walpole introduced both the Licensing Act and the Lord Chamberlain deliberately to suppress it. But Gay's intentions are clear because he published the play at his own expense: Macheath is transported to the West Indies where he blacks up and assumes the persona of a Caribbean pirate, Morano. In this role

he supports a slave revolt and becomes emotionally close to Chief Cawwawkee, the leader of the slave revolt. They have a passionate duet in which they melt into each other's arms; so no ambiguity there. Meanwhile the desolate Polly, disguised as a boy, follows her transported lover to the West Indies. Here she meets Jenny Diver who has also been transported and they two fall in love and have the English stage's first lesbian kiss, thus beating *Brookside* by over 200 years.

Gay's own sexuality remains shrouded. But he never married, never owned a house, apparently never had a girlfriend and all his best friends, Pope, Swift and Arbuthnot were male. Gay's first job in London was as a draper's assistant and one of his last plays, *Achilles*, depicted the eponymous hero not as a ferocious warrior but as a curious androgyne, happier dressing in petticoats and silks than armour and easier sewing with the girls than fighting the boys.

However, one charge I am open to is that Out of Joint are having a second bite of the convict cherry. I read Robert Hughes' brilliant *The Fatal Shore* when I was about to direct *Our Country's Good* and this has since prompted me to read more widely about transportation and the fascinating and neglected subject of early Australian history. *The Sydney Morning Herald*'s review of *Our Country's Good* was brilliant. The headline said "Daring Poms Pinch Our History." Well, we're back for a second raid! The famous dictum is that *The Beggar's Opera* made Gay rich and Rich, the manager of Drury Lane, gay. Well, our hope is that *The Convict's Opera* may make Gay gayer and the rest of us wiser.

CONVICTS, BEGGARS AND TRANSPORTATION
Iain Sinclair

Not all convict transportations were as horrific as the infamous second fleet. In fact after Earl Grey introduced surgeons on board, conditions were significantly better than the hulks they had been languishing in. For some, transportation meant their first access to medical care, clothing and education. On some transports even rum and beer were standard allocations in convict rations.

One in six convicts were women.

The youngest convict was nine and the eldest was 68.

The only successful mutiny on board a convict transport was the Lady Shore in 1796. It was carrying 66 women and one man, an adventurer, mercenary, scoundrel and all-round swashbuckler "Major Sempel Lisle". Lisle conspired with the civilian guards who were French, Irish, Danish and English.

The majority of highwaymen hanged in Tyburn were butchers or butcher's apprentices.

Very few convict transports contained actual British soldiers. Most of the time, the guards were recruited by a civilian contractor. It was not uncommon for guards, surgeons and even clergymen to dance, sing and party with their charges below.

No convicts ever succeeded in taking over any transport ship. In the case of The Lady Shore, the guard was made up of a number of French and Irish deserters who mutinied in the name of "liberty" but distributed the convict cargo as servants among the Spanish ladies of Rio de la Plata (in Uruguay).

The first Australian bushranger was John Caesar, an African slave who escaped from the West Indies to London and was sentenced in Kent for stealing 240 shillings. He escaped from the colony in Sydney many times and made his living stealing food from the colonists and indigenous alike. His nickname was "Black Caesar".

Jesse James and Ned Kelly were both fans of the legendary Jack Sheppard on whom Macheath is part based. Jesse James would even sign his letters "Jack Sheppard"

Peachum was inspired by the infamous thief-taker, Jonathan Wild "the father of organised crime" You can still go and visit his skeleton on display at the Royal College of Surgeons in Lincoln's Inn Fields.

THE BEGGAR'S OPERA
John Bull

When John Gay wrote to his friend Jonathan Swift that he was planning to write what he called, after the notorious London prison, a "Newgate pastoral", he can have had no idea that he was about to produce what would become the largest box-office hit of the eighteenth century.

First produced in 1728, it proved an immediate success and was subsequently frequently revived, through to the present day. Not only that, but he incidentally introduced a new theatrical genre, the ballad opera, that has a considerable claim as one of the antecedents of the modern popular stage musical. The music that Gay made use of was not original, though his lyrics largely were. He borrowed from the more well-known sections of contemporary operas but, above all, he drew from a tradition of popular ballads: one of the highpoints of *The Beggar's Opera* musically is the duet, "Over the Hills and Far Away", sung by the play's chief protagonists. The alliance of the sentimental heroine, Polly Peachum, with the swaggering highwayman, Macheath, loses nothing by Gay's resolute sending-up of their relationship. Newly wed, but with five other wives and assorted children in the wings, his first words to her in the play, "Suspect my honour, my courage, suspect anything but my love," are easily accepted by Polly: "I have no reason to doubt you, for I find in the Romance you lent me, none of the great Heroes were ever false in love".

Just as the conventions of sentimental and heroic romance are burlesqued, so are those of the contemporary Italian and French operas. So, at the end of the play, imprisoned after being betrayed, like Christ, with a kiss from Jenny Diver, one his tavern associates, "Maheath is to be hang'd": however, the player successfully opposes this, arguing that a moral conclusion is not in order "for an opera must end happily". Thus, its very construction as a ballad opera, drawing from populist sources, and its location in the sort of lowlife arenas much favoured

by Hogarth, operate to debunk the pretensions of high culture as represented by the true operas and their well-heeled patrons. The satire extends further, however. That is should have been so successful then and later is, in itself, a clue to the reasons for its popularity. It combined themes were both of strong contemporary relevance and capable of being applied to almost any set of social and political circumstances. For, *The Beggar's Opera* was above all conceived of as a political satire.

After the restoration of Charles II in 1660, real political power slowly but inexorably moved away from the monarchy and towards parliament. By the time of Gay's opera, the origins of the modern party system were in place, and opposition to the ruling government was no longer seen automatically as treason. In the latter half of the seventeenth century the two necessary institutions for the development of Britain as a capitalist nation were formed, the Bank of England and the Stock Exchange, and the City of London began to develop as a major financial centre. These city interests are represented in *The Beggar's Opera* by Peachum (the criminal gang-leader, fence and grass) and Lockit (the prison turnkey), the middle-men of the urban world of crime. Their world-view is well summed up by Peachum's "Of all animals of prey, man is the only sociable one – Every one preys upon his neighbour, and yet we herd together".

They are opposed by Macheath and his gang of courtier/highwaymen whose territory is the country and the open road. Ideologically, they are equatable with the old Tory values of land and succession, and see themselves as kind of latter-day Robin Hoods: "we are for a just partition of the world, for every man hath a right to enjoy life".

But Gay also has a more specific target in mind. After the first great scandal of the burgeoning capitalist state, the "South Sea Bubble" of 1720, the Whig politician Robert Walpole had risen to become Great Britain's first "Prime Minister". For the first time an organised legal opposition was formed both inside and outside Parliament, and Gay and his friends Alexander Pope and Jonathan Swift became vocal adherents of what came to be known as the Country Party. From the outset Gay's opera was rightly seen as an attack on the "great man" – an allusion to Walpole's size as well as to the power he wielded – and the Prime Minister had its sequel, *Polly*, banned from performance.

However, Gay's attack is more on what he saw Walpole representing, an unbrave new world of capitalism and corruption, than on the man himself. It is for this reason that – much like Gilbert and Sullivan's *Mikado* – the play has proved amenable to constant revival and subtle, and not so subtle, alterations to make it fit different party political situations. It also helps to explain how Bertolt Brecht should have borrowed something of the theatrical structure and some of the characters' names for his *The Threepenny Opera* which premiered just two hundred years after Gay's original. But, whereas Brecht's play concerns itself not only with criminals but with the world of beggars, Gay's actually does not. It is not about beggars, but by a beggar, Gay himself, impoverished, along with a substantial percentage of the population, by his financial dabblings in the South Sea Company. Gay's beggar only appears in the Prologue and towards the end of the play, not as a part of the action but as a commentator on it. *The Beggar's Opera* having, as contemporary punning had it, made the owner of the theatre "[John] Rich gay, and Gay rich". In *Polly* the action is no longer introduced by a beggar, but by the poet.

In the sequel, which as result of its banning Gay never lived to see performed, the characters are transported as convicts to the West Indies. Although the format remains much the same, the satire of the original is pushed much further. Now at the head of a band of pirates, Macheath blacks himself up to evade recapture – an ironic measure as he now embodies all the worst features of a corrupt western civilisation – and he is opposed by the leader of the native Indians, Cawwawkee, a version of the eighteenth century "Noble Savage" who is a model of moral decorum and courage. The effect is to give a greater emphasis to the proto-egalitarian impulses raised in *The Beggar's Opera*, but thwarted by Macheath's belated realisation that "the world is all alike, and that even our Gang can no more trust one another than other people". This time the happy ending is slightly deferred. Polly, having disguised herself as a young man to pursue a Macheath now declaredly married to the Jenny Diver who had previously betrayed him, greets the news that her man has been executed with the promise, after a decent interval has elapsed, of marriage to Cawwawkee. Gay's touch may be lighter but in *Polly* the attack on the supposed superiority of enlightenment Europe has echoes of Swift's gloomy conclusions about mankind in the final book of *Gulliver's Travels*, a work that also juxtaposes local satire with larger political themes.

John Bull is Professor of Film and Theatre at the University of Reading (UK) and author of, amongst other books, a work on the post-Restoration playwrights Vanbrugh and Farquhar.

THE CONVICT'S OPERA

Stephen Jeffreys

Adapted from *The Beggar's Opera* by John Gay

Dramatis Personae

On board the ship

WILLIAM VAUGHAN,
 director of the play

BEN BARNWELL,
 a coin clipper

BETT ROCK,
 a confidence trickster

HARRY MORTON,
 a man of mystery

GRACE MADDEN,
 an arsonist

TOM JENNER,
 a poacher

PHEBE GROVES,
 a pamphleteer

AMELIA WHITING,
 a thief

EDDIE COSGROVE,
 a political prisoner

BARTLEMY WILKINS,
 a clergyman

CAPTAIN MACNAUGHTON,
 the ship's captain

*Guards, sailors, convicts,
musicians*

In The Beggar's Opera

JOHN GAY, MRS VIXEN,
MATT OF THE MINT

PEACHUM,
BETTY DOXY

MRS PEACHUM,
MRS COAXER

MACHEATH

POLLY PEACHUM,
SUKY TAWDRY

FILCH,
JENNY DIVER

DIANA TRAPES,
THE HARPER

LUCY LOCKIT,
DOLLY TRULL

LOCKIT,
MRS SLAMMEKIN

A PLAYER, BEN BUDGE,
MOLLY BRAZEN

*This text went to press before the end of rehearsals and so may
differ slightly from the play as performed.*

PART ONE

Prologue

Darkness. The sound of a ship ploughing through heavy water. Then the raucous singing of convicts at night.

SONG – *to the tune of 'Sailing' by Gavin Sutherland.*

ALL.
>We are sailing, we are sailing,
>Bound in irons across the sea,
>We are sailing distant waters,
>Never more will we be free.
>
>We are flying, we are flying,
>Like a flock across the sky,
>You may watch us heading southwards,
>Searching for a place to die.
>
>Can you hear us, can you hear us,
>As we sing our joy and pain?
>We are searching for a new land,
>Where we may be born again.

Two bewigged gentlemen appear.

PLAYER. Sure, it cannot be. Mr Gay? The author of the celebrated *Beggar's Opera*.

JOHN GAY. Indeed, sir, it is none other.

PLAYER. But I had understood you dead and buried in Westminster some eighty years past.

JOHN GAY. An error, sir, albeit of my own devising. For, preferring to be interred in the flush and majesty of my fame to creeping when long forgotten into a pauper's tomb without an epitaph, I played a trick upon death's earthly henchmen and secured myself, for all eternity, a corner of the Abbey.

PLAYER. But you live yet? You are above one hundred and twenty years old.

JOHN GAY. It is not a remarkable occurrence in a poet. For ours is a solitary profession. Alone in our garrets, we fall not prey to the dropsies of the mob; nor are we run down by carts or choked on vapours in the pursuit of our trade like your bricklayer or hatter. No man ever drowned in his own inkwell.

PLAYER. Then what make you here on a convict ship bound for Australia? Why do you squander a lifetime's caution on such a hazard?

JOHN GAY. Folly and negligence, sir. For, searching the clutter-room of my brain for a simile and finding none, I stepped into the street to see if observation of life could provide where fancy failed. I was immediately apprehended by the watch for loitering, summoned before a gentleman with a wig and a malevolent aspect, and placed aboard this vessel.

PLAYER. Still, you have survived our perilous voyage, for our good captain informs us that land will be spied before the ending of our play.

JOHN GAY. Is there to be a play?

PLAYER. Indeed, Mr Gay, and not any play: it shall be your play, *The Beggar's Opera*.

JOHN GAY. Performed by convicts?

PLAYER. Indeed.

JOHN GAY. I trust they do not take the liberties with my words they took with the property of others.

PLAYER. Sure no, for the reforming power of punishment is at work on them already. Five long months aboard a crowded brig, their flesh scoured with the marks of disease and the lash, their bellies empty and their prospects bleak have elevated their spirits. They now comprehend the error of their ways and would no more steal a couplet from you than they would relieve a bishop of his ring and mitre.

JOHN GAY. I am glad to hear it.

PLAYER. So generous are they grown, they may well donate some of their own fancies to swell your store.

JOHN GAY. Such magnanimity I might well forego. But a half-dead poet with no better prospect than a grave in Sydney would fare best to acknowledge your charity in bringing his play on the stage than carp for being abridged.

PLAYER. Indeed. It is time for us to withdraw; the actors are preparing to begin. Play away the overture.

They go. MUSICIANS *come on, playing the overture. The play is being performed on a transportation ship by a cast of* CONVICTS *for the ship's company.*

ACT ONE

Scene One

PEACHUM*'s house.* PEACHUM *sitting at a table with a large book of accounts before him.*

AIR I – *An old woman clothed in gray, etc.*

PEACHUM.
>   Through all the Employments of Life
>   Each Neighbour abuses his Brother;
>   Whore and Rogue they call Husband and Wife:
>   All Professions be-rogue one another:
>   The Priest calls the Lawyer a Cheat,
>   The Lawyer be-knaves the Divine:
>   And the Statesman, because he's so great,
>   Thinks his Trade as honest as mine.

A Lawyer is an honest Employment, so is mine. Like me he acts in a double Capacity, both against Rogues and for 'em. 'Tis fitting we should protect and encourage Cheats, since we live by them.

Scene Two

PEACHUM, FILCH.

FILCH. Sir, Black Moll hath sent word her Trial comes on in the Afternoon, and she hopes you will order Matters so as to get her off.

PEACHUM. Why does she not plea of pregnancy? To my certain Knowledge she hath taken every opportunity to fill her belly. But, as the Wench is very active and industrious, you may satisfy her that I'll soften the Evidence against her.

FILCH. Tom Gagg, sir, is found guilty.

PEACHUM. A lazy Dog! When I took him the time before, I told him what he would come to if he did not mend his Hand. This is Death without Reprieve and I will collect my fee for informing. (*Writes.*) For Tom Gagg, forty Pounds. Let Betty Sly know that I'll save her from Transportation, for I can get more by her if she stays in England.

FILCH. Betty hath brought more goods into our Lock to-year than any five of the Gang.

PEACHUM. If none of the Gang inform on her, she may, in the common course of Business, live a Twelve-month longer. I love to let Women scape. A good Sportsman lets the Hen Partridges fly, because the Breed of the Game depends upon them. Besides, here the Law allows us no Reward; there is nothing to be got by the Death of Women – except our Wives.

FILCH. 'Twas to Betty I was obliged for my Education. She hath trained up more young fellows to the Business than the Gaming table.

PEACHUM. Truly, Filch, thy Observation is right. We and the Surgeons are more beholden to Women than all the Professions besides.

AIR II – *The bonny gray-ey'd Morn, etc.*

FILCH.

  'Tis Woman that seduces all Mankind,
  By her we first were taught the wheedling Arts:

> Her very Eyes can cheat; when most she's kind,
> She tricks us of our Money with our Hearts.
> For her, like Wolves by Night we roam for Prey,
> And practise ev'ry Fraud, to bribe her Charms;
> For suits of Love, like Law, are won by Pay,
> And Beauty must be fee'd into our Arms.

PEACHUM. But make haste to Newgate, Boy, and let my Friends know what I intend; for I love to make them easy one way or other.

FILCH. I'll away, for 'tis a Pleasure to be the Messenger of Comfort to Friends in Affliction.

Scene Three

PEACHUM. But 'tis now high time to look about me for a decent Execution against next Sessions. A Register of the Gang, (*Reading*.) Crook-finger'd Jack. Let me see how much the Stock owes to his Industry; one, two, three, four, five Gold Watches, and seven Silver ones. A mighty clean-handed Fellow! Sixteen Snuff-boxes, five of them of true Gold. Six Dozen of Handkerchiefs, four silver-hilted Swords, half Dozen of Shirts, three Periwigs, and a piece of Broad-Cloth. Considering these are only the Fruits of his leisure Hours, I don't know a prettier Fellow. Harry Padington, a poor petty-larceny Rascal, without the least Genius; were he to live these six Months, he will never come to the Gallows with any Credit. Matt of the Mint; a promising sturdy Fellow, and diligent in his way and may raise good Contributions on the Public, if he does not cut himself short by Murder. Tom Tipple, a guzzling soaking Sot, who is always too drunk to stand himself, or to make others stand. A Cart is absolutely necessary for him. Robin of Bagshot, alias Gorgon, alias Bob Bluff, alias Carbuncle, alias Bob Booty.

Scene Four

PEACHUM, MRS PEACHUM.

MRS PEACHUM. What of Bob Booty, Husband? I hope nothing bad hath betided him. He's a favourite Customer of mine.

PEACHUM. I have set his Name down in the Black List, that's all, my Dear; he spends his Life among Women, and as soon as his Money is gone, one or other of the Ladies will hang him for the Reward, and there's forty Pounds lost to us for ever.

MRS PEACHUM. You know, my Dear, I never meddle in matters of Death; Women are bad Judges in these cases: they think every Man handsome who is going to the Gallows.

PEACHUM. Indeed you do.

MRS PEACHUM. But really Husband, you should not be too hard-hearted, for you never had a finer set of Men than at present. We have not had a Murder among them all, these seven Months.

PEACHUM. What a dickens is the Woman always a-whim-pering about Murder for? Murder is as fashionable a Crime as a Man can be guilty of. So, my Dear, have done upon this Subject. Was Captain MacHeath here this Morning for the Bank-Notes he left with you last Week?

MRS PEACHUM. Yes, my Dear; and though the Bank hath stopped Payment, he was so cheerful and so agreeable! Sure there is not a finer Gentleman upon the Road than the Captain! Is he rich?

PEACHUM. The Captain keeps too good Company ever to grow rich. Mary-bone and the Chocolate Houses are his undoing.

MRS PEACHUM. Really, I am sorry upon Polly's Account the Captain hath not more Discretion. What Business hath he to keep Company with Lords and Gentlemen? He should leave them to prey upon one another.

PEACHUM. Upon Polly's Account! What a plague does the Woman mean? Upon Polly's Account!

MRS PEACHUM. Captain MacHeath is very fond of the Girl.

PEACHUM. And what then?

MRS PEACHUM. If I have any Skill in the Ways of Women, I am sure Polly thinks him a very pretty Man.

PEACHUM. And what then? You would not be so mad as to have the Wench marry him! Gamesters and Highwaymen are generally very good to their Whores, but they are very Devils to their Wives.

MRS PEACHUM. But if Polly should be in Love, how should we help her, or how can she help herself? Poor Girl, I am in the utmost Concern about her.

AIR IV – *Why is your faithful slave disdained? etc.*

> If Love the Virgin's Heart invade,
> How, like a Moth, the simple Maid
> Still plays about the Flame!
> If soon she be not made a Wife,
> Her Honour's sing'd, and then for Life
> She's – what I dare not name.

PEACHUM. Look ye, Wife. A handsome Wench in our way of Business is as profitable as at the Bar of a Temple Coffee-House, who looks upon it as her livelihood to grant every Liberty but one. You see I would indulge the Girl as far as prudently we can in anything, but Marriage! After that, my Dear, how shall we be safe? Are we not then in her Husband's Power? Polly is Tinder, and a Spark will at once set her on a Flame. Married!

MRS PEACHUM. Mayhap, my Dear, you may injure the Girl. She loves to imitate the fine Ladies, and she may only allow the Captain liberties in the view of Interest.

PEACHUM. But 'tis your Duty, your Duty, my Dear, to warn the Girl against her Ruin, and to instruct her how to make the most of her Beauty. I'll go to her this moment, and sift her. In the mean time, Wife, rip out the Coronets and Marks of these Dozen of Cambric Handkerchiefs, for I can dispose of them this Afternoon to a Chap in the City.

PEACHUM hands the handkerchiefs to MRS PEACHUM and goes off. WILLIAM VAUGHAN, the director of the play, appears, dressed in plain convict clothes with a fourteen-pound leg iron on his ankle.

WILLIAM. Thank you, Ben. That was well, very well.

Lights change. We're on the deck of the ship at night. The actor playing PEACHUM returns. He's a coin clipper called BEN BARNWELL. He is now out of costume and in convict clothes.

BEN. That line makes me melancholy.

WILLIAM. You miss the city?

BEN. Cowcross Street. Milk Street.

WILLIAM. Fetter Lane?

The actor playing MRS PEACHUM returns in convict clothes. She is a confidence trickster called BETT ROCK.

BETT. Fetters we still have. Have you decided?

WILLIAM. You were both very good.

BETT. So you haven't decided.

WILLIAM. We have time in abundance. I am making each part of the process last as long as possible.

BETT. I might get better offers.

WILLIAM. A rival company?

BETT. There might be.

WILLIAM. Two acting companies on a convict ship?

BETT. They might do *The Recruiting Officer*.

WILLIAM. That would not play well with convicts.

BETT. Might do, might do, might do.

WILLIAM. It's a chance I will take.

A FIGURE appears. All three become fearful.

FIGURE. What are you doing here?

WILLIAM. We have permission. Captain MacNaughton.

FIGURE. Your voices were strange to my ear.

WILLIAM. Who are you, friend?

The FIGURE *steps into the light. A man in his twenties, a convict in leg irons. His name is* HARRY MORTON. *Everyone relaxes a little at the sight of a fellow convict.*

HARRY. Very strange.

WILLIAM. How did you get permission to be on deck at night?

HARRY. Our whimsical captain. I heard you just now. You sounded as if you was speaking the thoughts of another.

WILLIAM. I am to present a play with fellow convicts in the course of the voyage. I am selecting my actors – or, as we call it, auditioning.

HARRY. A play?

WILLIAM. Yes, a play. You know what a play is?

HARRY. I know what a convict ship is.

WILLIAM. As do we all, we have been three weeks aboard.

HARRY. Three weeks in port.

BEN. Grim enough to my mind.

HARRY. No, friend. Port is the paradise of the voyage. Port is the Garden of Eden. Once we are at sea, then you will know a convict ship.

WILLIAM. Friend. I think you are the sort who will take any chance to preach gloom.

HARRY. I am no preacher. I say what I know.

WILLIAM. I shall christen you. I shall call you Mr Mystery.

BETT. Mr Misery.

HARRY. I have done this voyage before.

BEN. Then, Mr Mystery, we defer.

HARRY. This will be no place for plays.

WILLIAM. There is a deal of time to pass. Five months.

HARRY. If we're lucky.

WILLIAM. If we're lucky. And it will pass slow. I was myself a player, in a small way. I persuaded the captain. There is no better way to cheat boredom than with a play.

HARRY. Let me introduce you to your companions to be. There will be Disease. There will be Hunger. There will be Cruelty. There will be Despair.

BETT. You are young to be on your second transportation.

HARRY. Started young.

BEN. The Australian colony? What is it like?

HARRY. On that I say nothing. Except that I took my first chance to leave it. As to your play: show me your cheery faces when we reach the Equator. If you are still full of joy then, I will believe in your play. (*He turns to go.*) Have you done for now? Or is there more?

WILLIAM. There could be more.

BETT. It is my speech.

WILLIAM. Then. Let us hear it.

BEN *holds up a lantern on a pole so that* BETT *may read.* WILLIAM *listens.* HARRY *stands apart.* BETT *reads from a paper.*

Scene Five

MRS PEACHUM. Never was a Man more out of the way in an Argument than my Husband! Why must our Polly differ from her Sex, and love only her Husband? And why must Polly's Marriage, contrary to all Observation, make her the less followed by other Men? All Men are Thieves in Love, and like a Woman the better for being another's Property.

BETT *looks up.*

HARRY. Is that all?

BETT. Another actor must come on and we have none.

HARRY. I would see more. (*To* BEN.) Can you not play it?

BEN. It is too slight a role for me. Juvenile.

HARRY. Do you have the words written?

WILLIAM. Can you read?

HARRY. To my own satisfaction.

WILLIAM. Then here are words. I had a copy and I have made
  two more while we have languished in port.

HARRY. Slow work.

WILLIAM. But good work. The character is a young thief by
  the name of Filch.

HARRY. Filch. That's good. Filch is good.

  HARRY *scans the lines and acts the part tentatively.*

Scene Six

MRS PEACHUM. Come here, Filch. I am as fond of this Child,
  as though he were my own. He hath as fine a Hand at picking
  a Pocket as a Woman, and is as nimble-finger'd as a Juggler.
  If an unlucky Session does not cut the Rope of thy Life, I
  pronounce, Boy, thou wilt be a great Man in History. Where
  was your Post last Night, my Boy?

FILCH. I ply'd at the Opera, Madam; and considering 'twas
  neither dark nor rainy, so that there was no great Hurry in
  getting Chairs and Coaches, made a tolerable Hand on't.
  These seven Handkerchiefs, Madam. And this Snuff-box.

MRS PEACHUM. Set in Gold!

HARRY *makes a quantum leap. He understands who* FILCH *is and goes for it. It's not great acting but it is scene-stealing.*

FILCH. I had a fair Tug at charming Gold Watch. Pox take the Tailors for making the Fobs so deep and narrow! It stuck and I was forc'd to make my Escape under a Coach. I fear I shall be cut off in the Flower of my Youth, so that every now and then I have Thoughts of taking up and going to Sea.

MRS PEACHUM. Going to Sea, Filch, will come time enough upon a Sentence of Transportation. But hark you, my Lad. Don't tell me a Lye; for you know that I hate a Liar. Do you know of anything that hath pass'd between Captain MacHeath and our Polly?

FILCH. I beg you, Madam, don't ask me; for I must either tell a Lye to you or to Miss Polly; for I promis'd her I would not tell.

MRS PEACHUM. But when the honour of our family is concern'd –

FILCH. I shall lead a sad Life with Miss Polly, if she ever comes to know that I told you.

MRS PEACHUM. Yonder comes my Husband and Polly. Come, Filch, and tell me the whole Story. I'll give thee a most delicious Glass of a Cordial.

BETT *stops acting. Everyone looks at* HARRY. *Eventually:*

BEN. Mr Mystery. Flash boy, ain't he?

WILLIAM. Good. Very strong.

BETT. A little too strong for Filch, in my opinion.

HARRY. I enjoyed it.

BETT. We could all see that.

BEN. Yes, we saw you enjoying it, flash boy.

An uncomfortable moment as they size up HARRY.

WILLIAM. Well, thank you, Bett, thank you, Ben. Our allotted time has expired. Back to our confinement.

BETT. Not yet. I wish to know.

WILLIAM. Know what?

BETT. Whether the part is mine or not.

WILLIAM. A little time and ye shall see.

BETT. That is not good enough. You choose me now or not at all.

WILLIAM. In the profession, that is not the way we proceed.

BETT. But in my profession it is. I am on offer now. Do you want me?

A GUARD *appears.*

GUARD. All below.

BEN. Me too. I do not love the way you hold power of decision on us.

WILLIAM. I would prefer to sleep on it.

BEN. Sleep? What sleep will you get? Hatches down. The stink. The noise. The prowling in the dark.

WILLIAM. A little more reflection.

GUARD. These privileges can easily be withdrawn.

BEN. I want to know.

BETT. And me.

The pressure from BEN *and* BETT *even interests the* GUARD.

WILLIAM. Very well.

BETT. To both of us?

WILLIAM. Yes, to both of you.

BETT *goes down into the hold.* BEN *follows her. A brief moment between* HARRY *and* WILLIAM.

Can you sing?

HARRY. A little.

WIILLIAM. Think of a song tonight. And sing it for me tomorrow. There is a part called MacHeath.

HARRY. Is it a good part?

WILLIAM. It is the best part.

> WILLIAM *goes below.* HARRY *preens himself briefly. The*
> GUARD *catches this. The* GUARD *spits on* HARRY*'s*
> *shoes.*

GUARD. Below, scum.

> HARRY *obeys, the* GUARD *follows.*
>
> *Immediately, it's daylight. The weather is better.*

Scene Seven

PEACHUM, POLLY.

POLLY. I know as well as any of the fine Ladies how to make
the most of myself. A Woman knows how to be mercenary,
though she hath never been in a Court or at an Assembly. We
have it in our Natures, Papa. If I allow Captain MacHeath
some trifling Liberties, I have this Watch and other visible
Marks of his Favour to show for it.

AIR VI – *What shall I do to show how much I love her, etc.*

> Virgins are like the fair Flower in its Lustre,
> Which in the Garden enamels the Ground;
> Near it the Bees in play flutter and cluster,
> And gaudy Butterflies frolick around.
> But, when once pluck'd, 'tis no longer alluring,
> To Covent-Garden 'tis sent (as yet sweet),
> There fades, and shrinks, and grows past all enduring
> Rots, stinks, and dies, and is trod under feet.

PEACHUM. You know, Polly, I am not against your toying and
trifling with a Customer in the way of Business. But if I find
out that you have play'd the Fool and are married, you Jade
you, I'll cut your Throat, Hussy. Now you know my Mind.

Scene Eight

PEACHUM, POLLY, MRS PEACHUM.

AIR VII – *Oh London is a fine town.*

MRS PEACHUM (*in a very great passion*).
>   Our Polly is a sad Slut! nor heeds what we have taught
>   her.
>   I wonder any Man alive will ever rear a Daughter!
>   For she must have both Hoods and Gowns, And Hoops to
>   swell her Pride,
>   With Scarfs and Stays, and Gloves and Lace; And she will
>   have Men beside;
>   And when she's drest with Care and Cost, All tempting,
>   fine and gay,
>   As Men should serve a Cowcumber, she flings herself
>   away.

You Baggage! you Hussy! you inconsiderate Jade! had you
been hang'd, it would not have vex'd me, for that might have
been your Misfortune; but to do such a mad thing by Choice!
The Wench is married, Husband.

PEACHUM. Married! Do you think your Mother and I should
have liv'd comfortably so long together, if ever we had been
married? Baggage!

MRS PEACHUM. Can you support the Expence of a Husband,
Hussy, in Gaming, Drinking and Whoring? Have you Money
enough to carry on the daily Quarrels of Man and Wife about
who shall squander most?

PEACHUM. Let not your Anger, my Dear, break through the
Rules of Decency. Tell me, Hussy, are you ruin'd or no?

MRS PEACHUM. With Polly's Fortune, she might very well
have gone off to a Person of Distinction. Yes, that you might,
you pouting Slut!

PEACHUM. Speak, or I'll make you plead by squeezing out an
Answer from you. (*Pinching her.*) Are really bound Wife to
him?

POLLY (*screaming*). Oh!

MRS PEACHUM. How the Mother is to be pitied who has handsome Daughters! Lock, Bolts, Bars, and Lectures of Morality are nothing to them.

PEACHUM. Why, Polly, I shall soon know if you are married, by MacHeath's keeping from our House.

WILLIAM comes on.

WILLIAM. There is a question to consider. Peachum and his wife. Are they both angry with their daughter, I mean, equally angry? Perhaps Mrs Peachum is less angry because she, in her youth, has made the same mistakes that Polly does.

BETT. That would make her more angry. At least it would make me more angry.

A sound from below. WILLIAM and BETT turn and watch as a group of CONVICTS, almost the entire company of the play, appears. They all wear irons. They are followed by CAPTAIN MACNAUGHTON, a severe Scot who carries a roll of paper.

MACNAUGHTON. Line up!

The CONVICTS form a line. MACNAUGHTON addresses them.

You! All of you! Listen or be double damned. You are to rehearse and perform a play for your recreation and education. I would not normally hold with such fripperies. But although this is my first voyage as captain, it is my fourth as an officer and I have seen what boredom does. So. The following regulations shall be observed: (*Gets out his scroll and reads.*) One: Rehearsal shall take place in the half hour immediately following the convicts' exercise period. Additional rehearsals may be granted in the half hour after your fellow prisoners are below hatches for the night, dependent on good behaviour. An armed guard will attend all rehearsals. No imitation of lewd behaviour in the rehearsal of the play shall be tolerated. Likewise, there shall be no blasphemy and no insertion of scurrilous material like to promote a mutiny. (*He rolls up his scroll.*) So. You know where you stand. I will not linger.

Myself, I would favour a Bible-study class. But no Moses has
come forth to show you the way out of your intellectual captivity. If anyone has a mind to hurl himself over the side
during rehearsal, please do so this side of the Equator, then the
money I save on food will compensate for the loss of the
arrival bonus. Ha! You think I jest but I am, in fact, in earnest.

MACNAUGHTON *goes. A female convict,* GRACE
MADDEN, *is the first to break out of the line. She watches*
MACNAUGHTON *as he goes down the companionway.*

GRACE. He makes my piss run cold.

WILLIAM. Are we well met? Do we all know one another?

GRACE. What's the difference? We know why we're here.

BEN. I thought there were to be more of us.

WILLIAM. One more. It is a tradition when the company meets
for each to make himself known to the others. I am William
Vaughan. Actor by trade. I shall stage the production and
sketch in some minor roles.

GRACE. Grace Madden. Playing Polly. Seven years for arson.
Which is setting fire to things, for those that don't know.

WILLIAM. It will suffice to give your name and the part you
have been assigned.

GRACE. Whoosh!

WILLIAM. Your offence is a matter for the authorities. When
we're in rehearsal, we put our crimes –

HARRY. Alleged crimes –

WILLIAM. – our alleged crimes, to one side.

GRACE. The first one was malice. After that it is passion. There
is nothing to compare. A drunk night gives you a queasy
morning. A man is done in three minutes. But a good blaze
stays with you for ever.

BEN. I am Ben Barnwell. I will give Peachum. So I suppose I
am to be this woman's father.

GRACE. Whoosh!

BEN. I am sentenced for coin clipping. I do not protest my innocence. But I believe the law should be changed so that my art might be properly admired.

HARRY. Harry Morton. Though some call me Mystery. MacHeath is my part. My offence… you may guess at.

SONG – *'I Fought the Law' by Sonny Curtis*.

BETT. Bett Rock. Rock by name, rock by nature. You may build on me, though none ever has. Mrs Peachum.

TOM JENNER *steps forward, a shy countryman*.

TOM. Tom Jenner. I done nothing like this afore. I can do voices. I can play tunes, cut capers. I will take a stab at Filch. I don't mind. I'm doing it to get out of the hold. I'm used to the air. I'm used to the air.

BEN. A Johnny Raw.

TOM. What's a Johnny Raw?

BEN. You are, yokel.

PHEBE GROVES, *intelligent, reserved, is next*.

PHEBE. Phebe Groves. Is all I'm saying.

AMELIA WHITING, *confident, a bit arrogant, speaks*.

AMELIA. Amelia. Lucy Lockit. I saw it done on the stage. So I know. And I don't like any liberties taken. Or talk of liberties.

WILLIAM. There'll be no liberties here, friend.

BEN. Why do you call everybody 'friend'?

WILLIAM. Because you are all my friends. Or will be.

AMELIA. 'Friend' is a prelude to liberties.

PHEBE. Leave him be. His heart is good.

A momentary stand-off between the two. Then another man emerges from below, EDDIE COSGROVE, *a passionate Irishman*.

EDDIE. I will not be spoken to in that manner. The guard feller. The way he gives it with the gob. I'll not stand for it. I'm no thief, I'm no murderer. My 'crime' is politics, and I say it is their politics which is the crime.

WILLIAM. Perhaps this is not quite the moment for –

EDDIE. It is always the moment. My family fought for a United Ireland – Protestants and Catholics side by side against the British. I had two brothers killed at Vinegar Hill and we lost, but it's not over. And they may shoot us, hang us and transport us, but we will have Vinegar Hill again, wherever in the world they take us. And next time we will win.

WILLIAM. Eddie Cosgrove. Who will play Lockit.

EDDIE. Because I know how the locks work. I have been on the wrong side often enough. So, I will show how it is from the other side. Poacher playing gamekeeper.

TOM. Now then.

The intervention is slight, but EDDIE *picks it up.*

EDDIE. Was that your crime? The pheasant under the jerkin? Mustn't do that, boy. The birds of the field, they don't belong to your sort, did you not know that?

TOM. I said nothing.

EDDIE. You said enough.

WILLIAM. I would like, time being short, to make a start. We have done the beginning of the play in audition. Perhaps we could pick up at Air number eight –

Another intervention from below. The new arrival is wildly out of place. He is a clergyman, BARTLEMY WILKINS.

BARTLEMY. Mr Vaughan?

WILLIAM. I am known as William, friend.

BARTLEMY. Mr Vaughan. I am not here by choice. The captain has taken a dislike to me. I am dependent on his whim. And his whim is that I be pressed into your play, which I do not like, and which, I am sure, you do not like, but the captain's whim is the captain's whim and there is an end.

WILLIAM. Friend. Who are you?

BARTLEMY. I shall state first who I am not, which is a convict. I am the Reverend Bartlemy Wilkins. I am to serve God in His newest country, and I must have my harpsichord, and this is the only ship that would carry my harpsichord, and that at an unreasonable price. And now the captain threatens me that, notwithstanding the monies I have paid, my harpsichord will be heaved into the brine unless I am a part of the play. I know he does it to distress me. He is an upstart midshipman seeking to impose authority. I have no redress. So we will make the best of it.

EDDIE. Preacher, poacher, political prisoner...

WILLIAM. We shall all make the best of it.

Something in WILLIAM*'s manner commands attention.*

This voyage will be hard. But we have, the ten of us, a common purpose. We will do our play. By God, we will do it to the best of our strength. And we will show them.

EDDIE. Show them what?

WILLIAM. What people can do.

Pause.

EDDIE. Well. I am with you. Friend.

WILLIAM. Then, Grace. You love to sing, do you not?

GRACE. It is my other delight.

AMELIA (*quietly to* BETT). Whoosh!

WILLIAM. Then lead us in Air number eight.

SONG – *to the tune of 'I Wanna Be Straight' by Ian Dury and The Blockheads.*

ALL.
    I wanna be straight, I wanna be straight
    I'm sick and tired
    Of glazing stars and nicking gold plate
    I'm a lurker and cheater, I've tickled the peter
    I've pricked the wicker and drawn the King's picture
    And gathered the bleater.

I wanna be straight, I wanna be straighter
It's the very last time
I've legged through the slime with a marjorie-prater
I've done with robbing and canting the dobbin
The diminishing way don't provide enough pay
To keep me from sobbing.

No more this rogue'll
Be hunting the fogle
It's go boy and go girl
Out of the world of crime.

I wanna be strong, as strong as a rock
I gathered the bolts
And hid the results right under my frock
I lived on the cross and gave not a toss
But now we all say that crime didn't pay
'Cos we worked at a loss.

My life has taught me
Not to be naughty
So please transport me
Unto a brand new world.

We wanna be straight, we wanna be straight
We're totally chuffed in a boat to be stuffed
And travelling freight
We involuntary sailors are not gonna fail you
We're gonna be straighter than straighter than straight
All the way to Australia.

The rest of the COMPANY *back away as* GRACE *launches
into her song, each getting out their copies of the play in
readiness.*

AIR VIII – *Grim king of the ghosts, etc.*

POLLY.
        Can Love be control'd by Advice?
        Will Cupid our Mothers obey?
        Though my Heart were as frozen as Ice,
        At his Flame 'twould have melted away.

        When he kist me so closely he prest,
        'Twas so sweet that I must have comply'd;

So I thought it both safest and best
To marry, for fear you should chide.

MRS PEACHUM. Then all the Hopes of our Family are gone
for ever and ever!

PEACHUM. And MacHeath may hang us in hope to get our
Daughter's Fortune.

POLLY. I did not marry him coolly and deliberately for Honour
or Money. I love him.

MRS PEACHUM. Love him! Worse and worse! I thought the
Girl had been better bred. Oh, Husband, Husband! My Head
swims! I can't support myself. Oh! (*Faints.*)

PEACHUM. See, Wench, to what a Condition you have reduc'd
your poor Mother! A glass of Cordial, this instant.

POLLY *goes out, and returns with it.*

Ah, Hussy, this is now the only Comfort your Mother has
left!

POLLY. Give her another Glass, Sir. My Mama drinks double
the Quantity whenever she is out of Order. This, you see,
fetches her.

MRS PEACHUM. The Girl shows such a Readiness, and so
much Concern, that I could almost find it in my Heart to
forgive her.

AIR IX – *O Jenny, O Jenny where hast thou been.*

O Polly, you might have toy'd and kist
By keeping Men off, you keep them on.

POLLY.
But he so teaz'd me,
And he so pleas'd me,
What I did, you must have done.

MRS PEACHUM. Not with a Highwayman, Slut!

PEACHUM. A Word with you, Wife. 'Tis no new thing for a
Wench to take a Man without Consent of Parents. You know
'tis the Frailty of Woman, my Dear.

MRS PEACHUM. Yes, indeed, the Sex is frail. But the first time a Woman is frail, she should be careful for then or never is the time to make her Fortune.

PEACHUM. Since what is done cannot be undone, we must all endeavour to make the best of it.

MRS PEACHUM. Well, Polly; as far as one Woman can forgive another, I forgive thee. Your Father is too fond of you, Hussy.

POLLY. Then all my Sorrows are at an end.

MRS PEACHUM. A mighty likely Speech in troth, for a Wench who is just married!

AIR X – *Thomas, I cannot, etc.*

POLLY.
> I, like a Ship in Storms, was tost;
> Yet afraid to put in to Land:
> For seiz'd in the Port the Vessel's lost,
> Whose Treasure is contreband.
> The Waves are laid, My Duty's paid.
> O joy beyond Expression!
> Thus, safe a-shore, I ask no more,
> My All is in my Possession.

PEACHUM. I hear Customers in t'other Room: Go, talk with 'em, Polly; but come to us again, as soon as they are gone.

POLLY *goes.*

Scene Nine

PEACHUM, MRS PEACHUM.

PEACHUM. I tell you, Wife, I can make this Match turn to our Advantage.

MRS PEACHUM. I am very sensible, Husband, that Captain MacHeath is worth Money, but I believe he hath two or three Wives already, and then if he should die, Polly's Dower would come into a Dispute.

PEACHUM. That is a Point which ought to be consider'd.

AIR XI – *A soldier and a sailor.*

> A Fox may steal your Hens, Sir,
> A Whore your Health and Pence, Sir,
> Your Daughter rob your Chest, Sir,
> Your Wife may steal your Rest, Sir,
> A Thief your Goods and Plate
> But this is all but picking,
> With Rest, Pence, Chest and Chicken;
> It ever was decreed, Sir,
> If Lawyer's Hand is fee'd, Sir,
> He steals your whole Estate.

The Lawyers are bitter Enemies to those in our Way. They don't care that any body should get a clandestine Livelihood but themselves.

Scene Ten

MRS PEACHUM, PEACHUM, POLLY.

POLLY. 'Twas only Nimming Ned. He brought in a Damask Curtain, a Hoop-Petticoat, a pair of Candlesticks, and one Silk Stocking, from the Fire that happen'd last Night. (*'As'* AMELIA.) Whoosh!

PEACHUM. There is not a Fellow that is cleverer in his way than Ned. But now, Polly, you are married?

POLLY. Yes, Sir.

PEACHUM. And how do you propose to live, Child?

POLLY. Sir, upon the Industry of my Husband.

MRS PEACHUM. What, is the Wench turn'd Fool? A High-wayman's Wife, like a Soldier's, hath as little of his Pay, as of his Company.

PEACHUM. And had not you the common View of a Gentle-woman in your Marriage, Polly?

POLLY. I don't know what you mean, Sir.

PEACHUM. Of being a Widow.

POLLY. But I love him, Sir; how then could I have Thoughts of parting with him?

PEACHUM. Parting with him is the whole Scheme and Intention of Marriage. The comfortable Estate of Widowhood, is the only Hope that keeps up a Wife's Spirits. Secure what he hath got, and have him peach'd the next Sessions.

POLLY. What, murder the Man I love! The Blood runs cold at my Heart with the very Thought of it!

PEACHUM. Fie, Polly! What hath Murder to do in the Affair? Since the thing sooner or later must happen, I dare say the Captain would prefer that we get the Reward for his Death than a Stranger. The Captain knows that as 'tis his Employment to rob, so 'tis ours to take Robbers; every Man in his Business. So there is no Malice in the case.

MRS PEACHUM. Ay, Husband, now you have nick'd the Matter. To have him peach'd is the only thing could ever make me forgive her.

AIR XII – *Now ponder well, ye parents dear.*

POLLY.
> Oh Ponder well! Be not severe:
> So save a wretched Wife!
> For on the Rope that hangs my Dear
> Depends poor Polly's Life.

MRS PEACHUM. What, is the Fool in Love in earnest then? Why Wench, thou art a Shame to thy very Sex.

POLLY. But hear me, mother. If you ever lov'd –

MRS PEACHUM. Those cursed Play-Books she reads have been her Ruin. One Word more, Hussy, and I shall knock your Brains out, if you have any.

PEACHUM. Keep out of the way, Polly, for fear of Mischief, and consider what is propos'd to you.

MRS PEACHUM. Away, Hussy. Hang your Husband, and be dutiful.

A GUARD *comes on.*

GUARD. That's it. Back below.

WILLIAM. Ladies and gentlemen, thank you, an excellent start.

GUARD. 'Ladies and gentlemen.' I like the way you give your-selves airs.

WILLIAM. It is the correct form of address.

GUARD. Some borrowed words, a few extra rags, and sud-denly you're not scum.

WILLIAM. Yes. Astounding but true.

Lights change. Some weeks have gone by and it's warmer.
PHEBE *comes on.*

PHEBE. If you are a political, you keep your mouth shut. You say you don't want to talk about your crime because you are innocent. But everyone says they're innocent, they reply. Indeed, you say, but it is particular with me. And you stay mum so that they don't look down on you. It is one thing to be caught stealing a sheep or a roll of taffeta. That can be understood. But for printing and distributing pamphlets? It is enough with the confinement, the disease, the punishments and the lice, without being thought insane. The run to Tenerife was not bad. Five weeks, but the weather was good and we could come up on deck to exercise and rehearse.

AMELIA *appears for rehearsal, followed by* BARTLEMY.
PHEBE *steps away from them, studying her lines.*

AMELIA. Reverend Wilkins. I wish to apologise. I was not friendly when you first joined us. I'm sorry for that. This voyage is hard. I feel the need now for a man of God.

BARTLEMY. It is very difficult for us all.

AMELIA. It is the nights.

BARTLEMY. The nights?

AMELIA. The noises. Every night, as soon as we are below in
the dark. The male convicts, the sailors, even the officers,
they break into the women's quarters. The sounds of the ship
are very loud, creaks, splashes, groaning timbers. But at
night I cannot hear them. With the noise of the rutting. Hour
upon hour, the thumps, the groans, the slapping of flesh on
flesh. I kneel and thank God I am not a part of it. To my ears,
it is the most miserable sound in the world.

BARTLEMY. You do well to pray, my child.

AMELIA. Thank you, Reverend Wilkins.

BARTLEMY. And I will pray for you.

AMELIA. Then I shall pray for you.

> AMELIA *smiles at him and goes to talk to* PHEBE.
> BARTLEMY *is left uncomfortable with his thoughts. The*
> COMPANY *assemble. There are rudimentary costumes and*
> *props.*

Scene Eleven

MRS PEACHUM, PEACHUM. POLLY *listening*.

MRS PEACHUM. The Thing, Husband, must and shall be done.
We must take have him peach'd the next Session without her
Consent. If she will not know her Duty, we know ours.

PEACHUM. But really, my Dear, it grieves one's Heart to take
off a great Man. I can't find it in my Heart to have a hand in
his Death. I wish you could have made Polly undertake it.

MRS PEACHUM. But in a Case of Necessity – our own Lives
are in danger.

PEACHUM. Then, indeed, we must make Gratitude give way
to Interest. He shall be taken off.

MRS PEACHUM. I'll undertake to manage Polly.

PEACHUM. And I'll prepare Matters for the Old Bailey.

SONG – *to the tune of the traditional folk song 'Keep Your Eyes on the Prize'*.

> Now MacHeath is bound in jail
> He's got no money to pay his bail
> Keep your eyes on the prize
> Hold on.

MRS PEACHUM.
> But when Jack Ketch lets MacHeath swing
> Then we'll hear the guineas ring
> Keep your eyes on the prize
> Hold on.

PEACHUM.
> Our daughter will be in misery
> To lose her husband on the tree
> Keep your eyes on the prize (*etc*.)

MRS PEACHUM.
> But he won't be so badly missed
> When she sees he's a bigamist (*etc*.)

PEACHUM.
> Only thing we did wrong
> Brought up our daughter too headstrong (*etc*.)

MRS PEACHUM.
> Only thing we'll do right
> Is watch that rope pull good and tight (*etc*.)
>
> Hold on, hold on
> Keep your eyes on the prize
> Hold on.

BOTH.
> River Thames is deep and wide
> Weave a shroud to dress a bride (*etc*.)
>
> Death comes quick and soothes our pain
> 'Cos someone always stands to gain (*etc*.)

Scene Twelve

POLLY. Methinks I see him already in the Cart, sweeter and more lovely than the Nosegay in his Hand! What Volleys of Sighs are sent from the Windows of Holborn, that so comely a Youth should be brought to the Tree! Even Butchers weep! Jack Ketch himself hesitates to perform his Duty, and would be glad to lose his Fee, by a Reprieve. What then will become of Polly! Shall I inform him of their Design, and aid him in his Escape? It shall be so! But then he flies, absents and I bar myself from his dear Conversation! If he keep out of the way, my Papa and Mama may in time relent. If he stays, he is hang'd, and then he is lost for ever! He lies conceal'd in my Room. My parents are abroad, I'll this Instant let him out.

POLLY *exits, then returns.*

Scene Thirteen

POLLY, MACHEATH.

AIR XIV– *Pretty Parrot, say.*

MACHEATH.
> Pretty Polly, say,
> When I was away,
> Did your Fancy never stray
> To some newer Lover?

POLLY.
> Without Disguise,
> Heaving Sighs, Doting Eyes,
> My constant Heart discover,
> Fondly let me loll!

MACHEATH.
> O pretty, pretty Poll.

POLLY. And are you as fond as ever, my Dear?

MACHEATH. Suspect my Honour, my Courage, suspect any thing but my Love. May my Pistols miss Fire, and my Mare slip her Shoulder while I am pursu'd, if I ever forsake thee!

POLLY. Nay, my Dear, I have no Reason to doubt you, for I find in the Romance you lent me, none of the great Heroes were ever false in Love.

AIR XV – *Pray, fair one, be kind*.

MACHEATH.
>My Heart was so free,
>It rov'd like the Bee,
>Till Polly my Passion requited;
>
>I sipt each Flower,
>I chang'd ev'ry Hour,
>But here ev'ry Flow'r is united.

POLLY. Were you sentenc'd to Transportation, my Dear, you could not leave me behind you, could you?

MACHEATH. Is there any Power, any Force that could tear me from thee? You might sooner tear a Pension out of the hands of a Courtier, a pretty Woman from a Looking-glass or a Fee from a Lawyer. To tear me from thee is impossible!

AIR XVI – *Over the hills and far away*.

>Were I laid on Greenland's Coast,
>And in my Arms embrac'd my Lass;
>Warm amidst eternal Frost,
>Too soon the Half Year's Night would pass.

POLLY.
>Were I sold on Indian Soil,
>Soon as the burning Day was clos'd,
>I could mock the sultry Toil
>When on my Charmer's Breast repos'd.

MACHEATH.
>And I would love you all the Day,

POLLY.

Every Night would kiss and play,

MACHEATH.

If with me you'd fondly stray

POLLY.

Over the Hills and far away.

Yes, I would go with thee. But oh! how shall I speak it? I must be torn from thee. We must part.

MACHEATH. How! Part!

POLLY. We must, we must. My Papa and Mama are set against thy Life. They now, even now are in Search after thee. They are preparing Evidence against thee. Thy Life depends upon a moment.

MACHEATH. Then part we must.

POLLY. But what pain it is! Can thy Polly ever leave thee? But lest Death my Love should thwart, fly hence, and let me leave thee. One Kiss and then – one Kiss – begone – farewell.

MACHEATH. My Hand, my Heart, my Dear, is so riveted to thine, that I cannot unloose my Hold.

POLLY. But my Papa may intercept thee, and then I should lose the very glimmering of Hope. A few Weeks, perhaps, may reconcile us all. Shall thy Polly hear from thee?

MACHEATH. Must I then go?

POLLY. And will not Absence change your Love?

MACHEATH. If you doubt it, let me stay – and be hang'd.

POLLY. O how I fear! how I tremble! – Go – but when Safety will give you leave, you will be sure to see me again; for till then Polly is wretched.

SONG – *'500 Miles' by The Proclaimers*.

They part, he at one door, she at another.

ACT TWO

Near Tenerife. The MEN *are rehearsing the tavern scene. The* WOMEN *are watching, bored.*

WILLIAM. Supposing we do this differently. Supposing only Ben and I, giving my little all as Matt, are on at the start, and then all the other men rush on at the words 'sound men and true'. That would be frightening, would it not?

GRACE (*sotto voce to* PHEBE). Not.

WILLIAM (*to* GRACE). What?

GRACE. What? Yes, exactly.

WILLIAM. Ready, Ben.

Scene One

A tavern near Newgate. BEN BUDGE *and* MATT OF THE MINT *at the table, with wine, brandy and tobacco.*

BUDGE. But pr'ythee, Matt, what is become of thy brother Tom? I have not seen him since my Return from Transportation.

MATT. Poor Brother Tom had an Accident – (*Mimes being hanged.*) this time Twelvemonth and he was accounted such a fine physical specimen he is now assisting the surgeons in medical research.

BUDGE. Death is, on occasion, an opportunity to rise in the world.

MATT. Indeed. But for the living it goes very hard, especially among our profession. Why are the Laws levell'd at us? Are we more dishonest than the rest of Mankind? What we win is our own by the Law of Arms, and the Right of Conquest.

BUDGE. Where on earth would you find such another set of Practical Philosophers, who to a Man are above the Fear of Death?

This is the new cue. The MEN *leap onstage. It's unimpressive.*

ALL. Sound Men, and true!

The WOMEN *in the audience cannot contain their laughter.*

WILLIAM. Thespians, please. Consideration for your fellow players.

GRACE. It ain't frightening.

EDDIE. Will you keep it shut!

TOM. First time we done it.

GRACE. You can't see it. You can't see it because you're in it. There's only five of you. And one of them is a vicar. That's not a gang.

WILLIAM. That's all we have been allowed. Six men and four women, including me. More was considered dangerous.

BETT. Gracie's right. I been there when the boys is plotting. There's got to be a mob.

WILLIAM. The captain is fearful. A big group of men with mock weapons. It could incite a mutiny.

EDDIE. Is it only mock weapons?

PHEBE. You should let us join in.

HARRY. What, women?

BARTLEMY. There cannot be women in the scene.

EDDIE. Unless they are carrying in the wine and brandy.

PHEBE. Not women as women. Women as men.

Pause.

BEN. Well, you can't have that.

BETT. Why not?

BEN. That's not right.

TOM. They all will laugh at that.

EDDIE. You want it to be frightening. Women is not frightening.

BETT. Do what you was doing.

EDDIE. What?

GRACE. Do what you was doing and we'll show you.

The MEN *look at* WILLIAM.

WILLIAM. All right.

The MEN *reluctantly backtrack to their previous positions.*
The WOMEN *go into a huddle.*

MATT. Are we more dishonest than the rest of Mankind? What
we win is our own by the Law of Arms, and the Right of
Conquest.

BUDGE. Where on earth would you find such another set of
Practical Philosophers, who to a Man are above the Fear of
Death?

The WOMEN *leap on, joining in the* MEN*'s line and*
entrance.

ALL. Sound Men, and true!

The MEN *are impressed,* BARTLEMY *and* TOM *actually*
frightened.

WILLIAM. Agreed. With everyone on stage, it's exciting.

HARRY. But it creates, to my mind, a problem.

WILLIAM. Yes, friend?

BEN. The costume.

BETT. Easy. We hitch up our dresses.

HARRY. A problem of consistency. If the women are to play
extra men in the gang, then, logically, the men should
portray women in the female gang.

A pause while this sinks in.

EDDIE. No. That's flat out. It's impossible.

BETT. Few scraps of material, easy.

EDDIE. I'm not talking about costume. I'm talking about me, a person of some seriousness, standing in front of an audience of brigands and cut-throats, wearing a skirt.

AMELIA. It's not right. It's not proper to see that.

HARRY. There's the vicar. He has had much practice with the cassock. And Tom, the Johnny Raw, he will be accustomed to the smock. William's an actor, will wear anything that suits him. There's only two of you will find it strange to feel fresh air up your legs.

GRACE. Be a laugh.

BEN. See. That's it. It's not equal. You play men and you become frightening, we play women to be laughed at.

BETT. Would that be a truth you have stumbled across there?

BARTLEMY. The women will play men to swell the numbers. Frightening and so on. But we do not seek such an effect with the female scene.

GRACE. Not frightening, no. You will join us in enticing the audience.

AMELIA. That would not be proper.

GRACE. Everything must be 'proper' with you! Except at night when a whole regiment of guards marches through you!

BARTLEMY. You will not speak of a fellow convict in this way. A sister in Christ. A woman of good character.

WILLIAM. That is enough. We cannot have raised voices in rehearsal. The guards will send us below.

BEN. Raised voices is easy, we just say we was acting.

WILLIAM. Let us decide as a group. There are three choices. Men shall only play men and women only women. Women shall play men but men shall not play women. And finally women shall play men and men shall play women.

TOM. My head's in a spin.

PHEBE. Is this to be a vote?

WILLIAM. If you care to put it that way.

BEN. Very well.

WILLIAM. Very well then. All ready. Those voting for no
dressing as the other sex.

AMELIA *and* TOM *raise their hands*.

Those who would allow women only to change their costume.

BARTLEMY, BEN *and* EDDIE *raise their hands*.

Those who wish both sexes to imitate each other.

HARRY, WILLIAM, BETT, GRACE *and* PHEBE *raise
their hands*.

Well. I venture to say that, in performance, it will please our
fellow convicts on the day.

*Immediately, we race forward in time to the actual
performance.*

BUDGE. But pr'ythee, Matt, what is become of thy brother
Tom? I have not seen him since my Return from
Transportation.

MATT. Poor Brother Tom had an Accident – (*Mimes being
hanged.*) this time Twelvemonth and he was accounted such
a fine physical specimen he is now assisting the surgeons in
medical research.

BUDGE. Death is, on occasion, an opportunity to rise in the
world.

MATT. Indeed. But for the living it goes very hard, especially
among our Profession. Why are the Laws levell'd at us? Are
we more dishonest than the rest of Mankind? What we win is
our own by the Law of Arms, and the Right of Conquest.

BUDGE. Where on earth would you find such another set of
Practical Philosophers, who to a Man are above the Fear of
Death?

The MEN *and* WOMEN *leap on. The sight of the* WOMEN *dressed as* MEN *thrills the* CONVICT AUDIENCE.

ALL. Sound Men, and true!

ROBIN. Of try'd Courage, and indefatigable Industry!

NED. Who is there here that would not die for his Friend?

PADINGTON. Who is there here that would betray him for his Interest?

MATT. Show me a Gang of Courtiers that can say as much.

BUDGE. We are for a just Partition of the World, for every Man hath a Right to enjoy Life.

BETT (*as highwayman*). And we deplore avarice!

MATT. Indeed! A covetous fellow, like a Jackdaw, steals for the sake of hiding it. These are the Robbers of Mankind, for Money was made for the Free-hearted and Generous, and where is the Injury of taking from another, what he hath not the Heart to make use of?

JEMMY. Our several Stations for the Day are fixt. Good luck attend us all. Fill the Glasses.

AIR XIX – *Fill every glass, etc.*

MATT.

    Fill ev'ry Glass for Wine inspires us,
    And fires us With Courage, Love and Joy.
    Women and Wine should Life employ.
    Is there ought else on Earth desirous?

CHORUS.

    Fill ev'ry Glass (*etc.*)

Scene Two

To them, enter MACHEATH.

MACHEATH. Gentlemen, well met. My Heart hath been with you this Hour: but an unexpected Affair hath detain'd me. No ceremony, I beg you.

MATT. We were just breaking up to go upon Duty. Am I to have the Honour of taking the Air with you, Sir, this Evening upon the Heath? I drink a Dram now and then with the Stage-coachmen in the way of Friendship and Intelligence; tonight there will be Passengers upon the Western Road, who are worth speaking with.

MACHEATH. I was to have been of that Party but –

MATT. But what, Sir?

MACHEATH. Is there any Man who suspects my Courage?

MATT. We have all been Witnesses of it.

MACHEATH. Or my Honour and Truth to the Gang?

MATT. I'll be answerable for it.

MACHEATH. In the Division of our Booty, have I ever shewn the least Marks of Avarice or Injustice?

MATT. By these Questions something seems to have ruffled you. Are any of us suspected?

MACHEATH. I have a fixed Confidence, Gentlemen, in you all, as Men of Honour, and as such I value and respect you. Peachum is a Man that is useful to us.

MATT. Is he about to play us any foul Play? I'll shoot him through the Head.

MACHEATH. I beg you, Gentlemen, act with Conduct and Dis-cretion. A Pistol is your last Resort.

MATT. He knows nothing of this Meeting.

MACHEATH. Business cannot go on without him. He is a nec-essary Agent to us. We have had a slight Difference, and till

it is accommodated I shall be obliged to keep out of his way.
But you must continue to act under his Direction. The
moment we break loose from him, our Gang is ruin'd.

MATT. As a Bawd to a Whore, I grant you, he is to us of great
Convenience.

MACHEATH. Make him believe I have quitted the Gang, which
I can never do but with Life. At our private Quarters I will
continue to meet you. A Week or so will probably reconcile us.

MATT. Your Instructions shall be observ'd. 'Tis now high time
for us to repair to our several Duties; so till the Evening we
bid you farewell.

MACHEATH. I shall wish myself with you. Success attend you.

The GANG *load their pistols, and stick them under their
girdles.*

AIR XX – *March in Rinaldo, with drums and trumpets.*

ALL.
Let us take the Road
Hark! I hear the Sound of Coaches!
The Hour of Attack approaches,
To your Arms, brave Boys, and load.
See the Ball I hold!
Let the Chymists toil like Asses,
Our Fire their Fire surpasses,
And turns all our Lead to Gold.

They go except for BEN.

BEN. You would call me a coiner. A judge would describe me
as a counterfeiter. But in the trade we give ourselves the title
of 'bitcull'. Your bitcull is, to your criminal classes, what
your cavalry is to the army. A cut above. It takes no skill to
cudgel a gent in an alley and cop his wad. But to fashion a
sixpenny piece, without benefit of machinery or royal assent.
Class. If I gave the whole pack of you a month you couldn't
come up with a single coin that would not provoke mirth in a
bottle shop in Bow. Now listen carefully. You get your fossil
– that's an iron mould – to make a print of a good coin in
coarse, wet sand. Don't forget to do both sides or you will

look a right jobbernowl. Then the tricky bit. Use finer sand to fill in the pores of the coarse sand. Otherwise your sixpence will look like it had the worms. Dry over a fire until done. Then you've got your cast. Melt your brass or tin in a crucible and screw the two sides together. (*Picks out an audience member.*) Pay attention! You have to make one in the interval or you won't get a drink. Finally, the refining process: if you're working with copper, a pinch of white arsenic will give you the exact shade of East Indian copper; with silver you'll need a drop of aqua fortis which brings the metal to the surface and gives it that convincing whitish tint. Got that? Now try doing it below the decks of a swaying ship, in the dark, chained up, guards watching you night and day, with improvised equipment on coinage you've never clapped eyes on before. We landed in Tenerife twelve hours ago, and I have already knocked out the price of a week's good living. Call me a bitcull. Or just call me God.

BEN goes. Immediately a religious procession appears. There's something not quite right about it. BETT, GRACE, AMELIA *and* PHEBE *appear, barefoot, clad in black and carrying heavy wooden crucifixes. They sing in Latin. They stop.*

BETT. It is not good enough. The trick will not work if anyone laughs. We are poor English penitents imprisoned for our beliefs, grateful to have half an hour in a Catholic country. The slightest smirk and we are dead meat.

AMELIA. My crucifix is too heavy.

BETT. It's meant to be heavy. It is as heavy as your sins! We will start at one end of the quay and Lieutenant Peel will pick us up at the other. This is not a play, this is acting for your livelihood. Now. Across the gangplank and be penitent!

The procession moves off, more successfully. WILLIAM *comes on dressed as* MRS VIXEN. *He's very convincing.* EDDIE *appraises him.*

EDDIE. No one will know.

WILLIAM. You think?

EDDIE. It's a certainty. You'll pass for a woman.

WILLIAM. You're very kind.

EDDIE. Me, the Vicar, the Johnny Raw, it is all too clear what is our sex. But you're different.

WILLIAM. I have taken some pains with my costume.

EDDIE. It's not just that.

WILLIAM. You're right. That's why I'm here. I had only a little success as an actor. As you get older, well, you must make a living some way.

EDDIE. We must all do that.

WILLIAM. They liked it. Well-to-do men. Bankers, married men, officials in the Navy. They would pay for a man who looked like a woman but was a man. But it always had to be in the open. Alleyways and so on. I was apprehended by the watch. Near Seven Dials, in the act, with a gentleman. But the gentleman was a judge and therefore not to be troubled by the law. Whereas I had to bear the burden for both of us. I was accused of his fob watch and purse when what I had had of him was more personal.

EDDIE. A judge?

WILLIAM. Yes.

EDDIE gives WILLIAM *an awkward hug.*

EDDIE. See. You're like me. You're a political.

WILLIAM. Am I? My love waits for me in a cottage in Bethnal Green. I will never see him again. He is strong but his hands are clumsy. He likes to look at the garden, but without me the garden will die. This year there will be no nasturtiums. That isn't political.

EDDIE. Isn't it?

The procession of PENITENTS *returns. They cross the gangway and onto the ship, still singing. At last they throw down their crucifixes. They drop heaps of foreign money onto the floor.*

PHEBE. Look at it! Look at it!

AMELIA. It's foreign, we don't know how much it is.

BETT. It is a lot.

GRACE. How do you know?

BETT. Because of the tears. They believed in us. They believed. Now. A cut for the Lieutenant. The rest is for us to get drunk!

AMELIA *and* PHEBE *run off, laughing.* BETT *is following them off until* GRACE *calls her.*

GRACE. Bett.

BETT *is surprised to see* GRACE *in tears.*

BETT. Don't be upset. Just 'cos you took their money. They're foreigners, they don't feel nothing.

GRACE. It's not that.

BETT. What then?

GRACE. You said as how you was a rock that could be built on.

BETT. Yes?

GRACE *rummages in her pockets and produces various items, which she hands to* BETT.

GRACE. Wadding. Dry splints of timber. A piece of cord with the end dipped in sulphur. Gunpowder. A tinderbox.

BETT *looks at her.*

Whoosh!

BETT. How d'you get these?

GRACE. Come on. Little favours here and there.

BETT. You thinking to set fire to the boat?

GRACE. I could have done it. Don't you think it was beyond me. Dry weather, that harpsichord would have taken.

BETT. Why you giving these to me?

GRACE. Take 'em from me. I don't want to do it. I thought it would be a favour. Put us all out of our misery. Take 'em.

BETT. You changed your mind. Why?

GRACE. Don't want to talk about it.

BETT. Why?

GRACE. Got shown some kindness.

GRACE *goes*. BETT *looks at the fire-raising kit*.

BETT. Whoosh!

Scene Three

MACHEATH *sits at the table, melancholy*.

MACHEATH. What a Fool is a fond Wench! Polly is most confoundedly bit. I love the Sex. And a Man who loves Money, might as well be contented with one Guinea, as I with one Woman.

AIR XXI – *Would you have a young virgin, etc*.

If the Heart of a Man is deprest with Cares,
The Mist is dispell'd when a Woman appears;
Like the Notes of a Fiddle, she sweetly, sweetly
Raises the Spirits, and charms our Ears,
Roses and Lilies her Cheeks disclose,
But her ripe Lips are more sweet than those.
Press her, Caress her, With Blisses, Her Kisses
Dissolve us in Pleasure, and soft Repose.

I must have Women. Nothing unbends the Mind like them. Money is not so strong a cordial.

Scene Four

The WOMEN *appear magically from every part of the stage as if* MACHEATH'*s thought has conjured them. The* MEN *of the company appear in drag with varying degrees of success alongside the real women:* BETT *as* MRS COAXER*;* AMELIA *as* DOLLY TRULL*;* WILLIAM *as* MRS VIXEN*;* BEN *as* BETTY DOXY*;* TOM *as* JENNY DIVER*;* EDDIE *as* MRS SLAM-MEKIN*;* GRACE *as* SUKY TAWDRY*; and* BARTLEMY *as* MOLLY BRAZEN.

MACHEATH. Dear Mrs Coaxer! You are welcome! You look charmingly to-day. Dolly Trull! Kiss me, you Slut; are you as amorous as ever, Hussy?

Business with TOM, *who resists.*

Ah Dolly, thou wilt ever be a Coquette! Mrs Vixen, I'm yours –

WILLIAM *is astonishingly at ease in his frock.*

I always lov'd a Woman of Wit and Spirit; they make charming Mistresses, but plaguey Wives. Betty Doxy! Come hither, Hussy. Do you drink as hard as ever?

BEN *plays this up.*

You had better stick to good wholesome Beer; for in troth, Betty, Strong-Waters will in time ruin your Constitution. What! And my pretty Jenny Diver too! As prim and demure as ever! There is not any Prude, though ever so high-bred, hath a more sanctify'd Look, with a more mischievous Heart. Mrs Slammekin!

EDDIE *looks the least female of all.*

As careless and genteel as ever! All you fine Ladies, who know your own Beauty, affect an Undress. But see, here's Suky Tawdry come to contradict what I am saying. Everything she gains from being on her back she lays out upon her Back. Why, Suky, you must keep at least a Dozen Talleymen. Molly Brazen!

BARTLEMY *kisses* MACHEATH.

That's well done. I love a free-hearted Wench. Thou hast a most agreeable Assurance, Girl, and art as willing as a Turtle. But hark! I hear Music.

The HARPER – *played by* PHEBE – *is at the door.*

If Music be the Food of Love, play on. Ere you seat your-selves, Ladies, what think you of a Dance? Come in.

Enter HARPER.

Play the French Tune, that Mrs Slammekin was so fond of.

A dance à la ronde *in the French manner; the* MEN *dance with an unexpected precision. Near the end of it:*

AIR XXII – *Cotillion.*

> Youth's the Season made for Joys,
> Love is then our Duty,
> She alone who that employs,
> Well deserves her Beauty.
> Let's be gay, While we may,
> Beauty's a Flower, despis'd in Decay,

CHORUS.
> Youth's the Season (*etc.*)

MACHEATH.
> Let us drink and sport to-day,
> Ours is not to-morrow.
> Love with youth flies swift away,
> Age is nought but Sorrow.
> Dance and sing, Time's on the Wing.
> Life never knows the Return of Spring.

CHORUS.
> Let us drink (*etc.*)

MACHEATH. Now, pray Ladies, take your Places. Here Madam.

Pays the HARPER, *who goes.* MACHEATH *waves bottles.*

If any of the Ladies choose Ginn, I hope they will be so free to call for it.

BETTY. My dear Sir. I would love to share a glass, but alas, my corset is biting into my flesh like a mating lobster. I must retire to give my middle parts a little respite.

MACHEATH. How forthright are the Ladies of our day! Happy unbuckling!

BEN *goes off for his quick change into* PEACHUM.

JENNY. Wine is strong enough for me. I hope, Mrs Coaxer, you have had good Success of late in your Visits among the Mercers.

COAXER. With Industry, one may still have a little Picking. I carried a length of silver-flower'd taffeta, and a square of black silk to Mr Peachum but last Week.

VIXEN. There's Molly Brazen hath the Ogle of a Rattle-Snake. She riveted a Linen-Draper's Eye so fast upon her, that he was nick'd of three Pieces of Cambric before he could look off.

BRAZEN. Oh dear Madam! But sure nothing can come up to your handling of Laces! And then you have such a sweet deluding Tongue! To cheat a Man is nothing; but the Woman must have fine parts indeed who cheats a Woman.

VIXEN. You are apt, Madam, to think too well of your Friends.

COAXER. If any Woman hath more Art than another, to be sure, 'tis Jenny Diver. Though her Fellow be never so agreeable, she can pick his Pocket as coolly, as if money were her only Pleasure.

JENNY. I never go to the Tavern with a Man, but in the View of Business. I have other Hours, and other sorts of Men for my Pleasure –

MACHEATH. Have done with your Compliments, Ladies, and drink about: Jenny. You are not so fond of me as you used to be.

JENNY. 'Tis not convenient, Sir, to shew my Fondness among so many Rivals. 'Tis your own Choice, and not my Inclination that will determine you.

AIR XXIII – *All in a misty Morning, etc*.

> Before the Barn-Door crowing,
> The Cock by Hens attended,
> His Eyes around him throwing,
> Stands for awhile suspended.
> Then one he singles from the Crew,
> And cheers the happy Hen;
> With how do you do, and how do you do,
> And how do you do again.

MACHEATH. Ah Jenny! Thou art a dear Slut.

TRULL. Pray, Madam, were you ever a kept woman?

TAWDRY. I have met with good fortune as well as my Neighbours.

TRULL. Pardon me, Madam, I meant no harm by the Question; 'Twas only in the way of Conversation.

TAWDRY. Indeed, Madam, I might have liv'd very handsomely with my last Friend. But upon his missing five Guineas, he turn'd me off. He was the kind who counted his money.

SLAMMEKIN. Who do you look upon, Madam, as the best sort of Man to keep a Woman?

TRULL. It depends not on the type but the individual.

SLAMMEKIN. I was once kept by a Money-Lender. Whenever he entered my Bedchamber, I would snaffle his Abacus: so he never knew what had merely been lent and what had been spent irrecoverably.

TAWDRY. For my Part, I own I like an old Fellow: for I always make him pay for what he can no longer do.

VIXEN. A spruce Prentice, Ladies, is no ill thing. Give him a prick, he will bleed Money.

JENNY. But to be sure, Sir, with so much Good-fortune as you have had upon the Road, you must be grown immensely rich.

MACHEATH. The Road, indeed, hath done me Justice, but the Gaming-Table hath been my Ruin.

SONG – *'Big Spender' by Cy Coleman and Dorothy Fields.*

JENNY. A Man of Courage should never put anything to the Risk but his Life.

She takes up his pistol. TAWDRY *takes up the other.*

These are the Tools of a Man of Honour. Cards and Dice are fit only for cowardly Cheats, who prey upon their Friends.

TAWDRY. This, Sir, is fitter for your Hand.

Handcuffs MACHEATH *and draws him close.*

You should not play with Dice for it takes you away from Women. How fond could I be of you! (*Casting him away.*) But before Company 'tis ill bred to slobber.

MACHEATH. Wanton Hussies!

JENNY. I must have a Kiss to give my Wine a Zest.

They take him about the neck. PEACHUM *rushes in upon him.*

Scene Five

PEACHUM. I seize you, Sir, as my Prisoner.

MACHEATH. Jenny? Women are Decoy Ducks; who can trust them! Jades, Jilts, Harpies, Furies, Whores!

PEACHUM. Your Case, Mr MacHeath, is not particular. The greatest Heroes have been ruin'd by Women. But, to do them Justice, I must own these are a pretty collection of Creatures. But you must now, Sir, take your Leave of the Ladies, and if they have a mind to make you a Visit, they will be sure to find you at your new home. This Gentleman, Ladies, lodges in Newgate. Captain, I'll wait upon you to your Lodgings. Ladies, I'll take care the Reckoning shall be discharg'd.

MACHEATH *is taken away by* PEACHUM, *but we see him being chained, stripped of his fine attire and led away during the following scene.*

Scene Six

VIXEN. Jenny: though Mr Peachum may have made a private Bargain with you and Suky Tawdry for betraying the Captain, as we were all assisting, we ought all to share alike.

COAXER. I think Mr Peachum, after so long an Acquaintance, might have trusted me as well as Jenny Diver.

SLAMMEKIN. He cheats us all. He hanged three Men last year who should have been set down to my Account.

TRULL. Mrs Slammekin, that is not fair. For you know the biggest of them was taken in Bed with me.

JENNY. As far as a Bowl of Punch or a Treat, I believe Mrs Suky will join with me. As for anything else, Ladies, you cannot in Conscience expect it.

So they must exit, but do so with exaggerated politeness.

SLAMMEKIN. Dear Madam –

TRULL. I would not for the World –

SLAMMEKIN. 'Tis impossible for me –

TRULL. As I hope to be sav'd, Madam –

SLAMMEKIN. Nay then, I must stay here all night –

TRULL. Since you command me.

Exeunt with great ceremony.

AIR XXV – *When first I laid siege to my chloris, etc.*

MACHEATH.
    At the Tree I shall suffer with Pleasure,
    At the Tree I shall suffer with Pleasure,
    Let me go where I will, In all kinds of Ill,
    I shall find no such Furies as these are.

Suddenly we are back in rehearsal. CONVICTS *in irons on a ship.*

WILLIAM. When we make a play we dream. And what do we convicts dream of? Imprisonment.

End of Part One.

PART TWO

Blackout. The whole COMPANY *starts to sing.*

SONG – *'Three Months on a Leaky Boat', to the tune of 'Six Months in a Leaky Boat' by Split Enz.*

WILLIAM *comes forward and harangues the audience returning from the interval.*

WILLIAM. Are there any virgins aboard ship? No, no, I do not mean that kind of virgin. Three months in a floating mixed dormitory and a stop in steamy Tenerife? Not likely. I mean the other kind. The ones who have never before crossed over. (*Pause.*) What a merry bunch of convicts you are. I mean the ones that have never before crossed over the Equator. Hands up if you've crossed the Equator. (*Looks around.*) Not in a plane! On sea. (*Looks at diminishing number of raised hands.*) That's better. (*Picks seasoned-looking audience member.*) Yes Sir/Madam, I could tell you were no virgin. With one solitary glance. Well, for that vast majority who are, in this one respect... intact... we will honour you with the ceremony of crossing the line.

Darkness. Gongs sound. Swaying lanterns light the scene. The COMPANY *emerge in fantastic costumes as* KING NEPTUNE *and his* NEREIDS *(his daughters). They are all drunk.* NEPTUNE *himself is bearded and cloaked in a porpoise skin, its snout pointing upwards to make him seem immensely tall. He carries a trident. His followers have dyed-red faces and wigs made from seaweed.*

They clatter and sway their way forward in a body, dangerously close to the audience.

An enormous volume is presented to NEPTUNE. *He inspects it closely, then looks towards a particular seat in the auditorium. All eyes turn towards the selected audience member – who is perhaps a plant. They advance on the unfortunate and enact the ritual of shaving, besmirching and immersion while singing the following song:*

ALL.

Those sailors first crossing the boundary line
Which is called by all seamen 'Equator'
Shall be tethered and lathered and ruthlessly barbered
Till a stranger to Mater and Pater
Then they're bothered and smothered and muddied and
    crudded
With all of the filth from our motions
And what better way to wash it away
Than be towed on a rope in the ocean.

For Neptune's the King, the King of the sea
And to him and his trident a penance is due
If your deck's orlop or quarter
The King and his daughters
Are sure to be forking with you.
Yes, we're sure to be forking with you!

The victim is released. A change. The entire COMPANY *except* HARRY *and* BETT *stretch out on the floor.* BETT *paces, unwell.*

BETT. After the Equator, the doldrums. The wind drops, the ship stops. A sailing ship that cannot sail is a fish in a desert. The shuddering motion of getting nowhere is worse for the seasickness than top speed. Too hot to move, too hot even to stand up. Everything is damp. Knives rust, leather goes white with mould, water is rationed even tighter than before. At such slow speeds we never escape our own filth, so everything stinks. One day we ended ten miles back from where we started. If only we could walk on water. Then we could bend our backs and drag the ship behind us on ropes. It would be quicker than the doldrums.

BETT *sinks to the deck with the rest.* HARRY *comes on.*

WILLIAM. Rehearsal.

No one moves.

We have a play to prepare.

EDDIE. Give a good man a taste of power and he becomes a
tyrant. There are no exceptions.

WILLIAM. This is mutiny. Rehearsal-room mutiny.

GRACE. So it is. Will you face us down, Captain?

A moment. WILLIAM *looks at his inert* COMPANY. *Then
walks away.*

Lighting change. TOM *in his fetters.*

TOM. It changes you. Being locked up. What is the captain's
word? 'Confinement.' I am confined. My space is not my
space, but their space. No more fields for Tom. No more
racing so hard across the morning meadow you feel you will
catch up with the birds. Fourteen-pound weight on your
ankle. You move slowly. The boat moves slowly. And yet we
are so long aboard this ship, you feel the change. I am
become sly. I no longer trust. I look into another's face and
think, what does he want out of me? And what can I get out
of him? Slowly we sail towards this country we do not know.
Except we know that when we reach it, there will be no need
of fetters, because the whole country will be a prison. Even
when you run free in the meadows, if there are meadows,
you will still be confined.

Scene Seven

Newgate. LOCKIT, MACHEATH.

LOCKIT. Noble Captain, you are welcome. You have not been
a Lodger of mine this Year and a half. You know the Custom,
Sir. Garnish, Captain, Garnish. Hand me down those Fetters
there.

MACHEATH. Those, Mr Lockit, seem to be the heaviest of all.
I should like the further Pair better.

LOCKIT. We have them at all Prices, from one Guinea to ten.

MACHEATH. I understand you, Sir. (*Gives him money.*) The fees here are so exorbitant, that few can bear the Expense of dying like a Gentleman.

LOCKIT. These will fit you better. Do but examine them, Sir. How genteely they are made! They will fit as easy as a Glove, and the nicest Man in England might not be asham'd to wear them. (*He puts on the chains.*) And so, Sir, I now leave you to your private Meditations.

Scene Eight

MACHEATH. To what a woeful Plight have I brought myself! Here must I be confin'd to hear the Reproaches of a Wench to whom I have promis'd marriage. I am in the Custody of her Father and if he knows of the matter, I shall have a fine time betwixt this and my Execution. But here comes Lucy, and I cannot get from her. Would I were deaf!

Scene Nine

MACHEATH, LUCY.

LUCY. You base Man. How can you look me in the Face? O MacHeath, thou hast robb'd me of my Quiet. To see thee tortur'd would give me Pleasure.

AIR XXVII – *A lovely lass to a friar came, etc.*

> Thus when a good Huswife sees a Rat
> In her Trap in the Morning taken,
> With Pleasure her Heart goes pit-a-pat,
> In Revenge for her loss of Bacon.
> Then she throws him to the Dog or Cat
> To be worried, crush'd and shaken.

MACHEATH. Have you no Tenderness, my dear Lucy, to see a Husband in these Circumstances?

LUCY. A Husband!

MACHEATH. In ev'ry Respect but the Form, and that, my Dear, may be said over us at any time. Friends should not insist upon Ceremonies. From a Man of Honour, his Word is as good as his Bond.

LUCY. 'Tis the Pleasure of all you fine Men to insult the Women you have ruin'd.

MACHEATH. I swear, the very first Opportunity, my Dear, you shall be my Wife in whatever manner you please.

LUCY. And so you think I know nothing of the Affair of Miss Polly Peachum. I could tear thy Eyes out!

MACHEATH. You can't be such a fool as to be jealous of Polly!

LUCY. You are married to her!

MACHEATH. Married! Very good. The Wench gives it out only to ruin me in thy good Opinion. 'Tis true, I go to the House; I chat with the Girl, I kiss her, I say a thousand things to her (as all Gentlemen do) to divert myself; and now the silly Jade hath set it about that I am married to her. These violent Passions may be of ill Consequence to a Woman in your Condition.

LUCY. Miss Polly hath put it out of your Power to do me the Justice you promis'd me.

MACHEATH. I will convince you of my Sincerity: find the Prison Chaplain and I shall make you my Wife; and I know the Consequences of having two at a time.

LUCY. Except you are about to be hang'd, and rid of us both.

MACHEATH. I am ready to give you Satisfaction. What can a Man of Honour say more?

LUCY. So then you are not married to Miss Polly.

MACHEATH. The Girl is prodigiously conceited. No Man can say a civil thing to her but her Vanity makes her think he's her own for ever and ever.

LUCY. Indeed so. She has ever been a monument to pride.

SONG – *to the tune of 'You're So Vain' by Carly Simon*.

> Oh she walked into the alehouse
> Like she was walking onto a barge
> Her dress was falling off her shoulder
> To give all the lechers a charge
> She had one eye in her looking glass
> As she shook her décolletage
> And all the men dreamed that they'd be her bedmate
> They'd be her bedmate, and...

CHORUS.
> She's so vain
> She'll probably think this song is about her
> She's so vain
> I'll bet she'll think this song is about her
> Won't she? Won't she?

LUCY.
> Well, I hear she went down to Epsom
> And her horse won by a head
> She gave some away and she kept some
> Like she does when men take her to bed
> And all the time she was hanging out
> With the flotsam and the jetsam
> Those underworld types
> Like my highwayman husband, highwayman husband.

CHORUS.
> She's so vain
> She'll probably think this song is about her
> She's so vain
> I'll bet she'll think this song is about her
> Won't she? Won't she?

MACHEATH. When Women consider their own Beauties, they are unreasonable for they expect their Lovers should like them as long as they like themselves.

LUCY. Yonder is my Father – perhaps through him we may light upon the Chaplain, who shall try if you will be as good as your Word.

Scene Ten

PEACHUM, LOCKIT *with a book of accounts*.

LOCKIT. Brother Peachum, we are agreed. You have consented to go halves in MacHeath.

PEACHUM. We shall never fall out about an Execution. How stands our last Year's Account?

LOCKIT. If you will run your Eye over it, you'll find 'tis fair and clearly stated.

PEACHUM. The Government's delay in paying us our due rewards is very hard! Do they expect us to hang our Acquaintances for nothing? Unless they pay more promptly, I shall let all the Rogues live.

LOCKIT. They treat us as if ours were not a reputable profession.

PEACHUM. In one respect our Employment may be reckon'd dishonest, because, like great Statesmen, we encourage those who betray their Friends.

LOCKIT. Such Language, Brother, anywhere else, might turn to your Prejudice.

AIR XXX – *How happy are we, etc*.

> When you censure the Age,
> Be cautious and sage,
> Lest the Courtiers offended should be:
> If you mention Vice or Bribe,
> 'Tis so pat to all the Tribe;
> Each cries – That was levell'd at me.

PEACHUM. Here's poor Ned Clincher's Name, I see. Sure Brother Lockit, there was a little unfair Proceeding in Ned's Case: for he told me in the Condemn'd Hold, that you had promis'd him a Session or two longer without Molestation.

LOCKIT. Mr Peachum: this is the first time my Honour was ever call'd in Question.

PEACHUM. Business is at an end if we act dishonourably.

LOCKIT. Who accuses me?

PEACHUM. You are warm, Brother.

LOCKIT. He that attacks my Honour, attacks my Livelihood
And this Usage – Sir – is not to be borne.

PEACHUM. Since you provoke me to speak I must tell you too,
that Mrs Coaxer charges you with defrauding her of her
Information-Money, for the apprehending of curl-pated
Hugh. Indeed, indeed, Brother, we must punctually pay our
Spies, or we shall have no Information.

LOCKIT. Is this Language to me, Sirrah, who have sav'd you
from the Gallows, Sirrah!

They collar each other.

PEACHUM. If I am hang'd it shall be for ridding the World of
an arrant Rascal.

LOCKIT. This Hand shall do the office of the Halter you
deserve, and throttle you, you Dog!

PEACHUM. Brother, Brother. We are both in the Wrong for
you know we have it in our Power to hang each other. You
should not be so passionate.

LOCKIT. Nor you so provoking.

PEACHUM. 'Tis our mutual Interest we should agree. If I said
anything, Brother, to the Prejudice of your Character, I ask
pardon.

LOCKIT. Brother Peachum, I can forgive as well as resent.
Give me your Hand. Suspicion does not become a Friend.

PEACHUM. I only meant to give you Occasion to justify yourself. But I must now step home, for I expect the Gentleman
about this Snuff-box, that Filch nimm'd two nights ago in the
Park. Good day.

On deck, day, just before rehearsals.

PHEBE. I know what you're thinking.

EDDIE. You do not.

PHEBE. I think I do.

EDDIE. Then describe my thought. Is it a good thought?

PHEBE. It is a hazardous thought.

EDDIE. Then you do know. How hazardous?

PHEBE. Very. A throw of the dice. Lose, you lose all.

EDDIE. Quite hazardous.

PHEBE. There is Ben the forger. He is a knowable man.

EDDIE. Straightforward, yes.

PHEBE. And there is Mr Mystery. He is an unknowable man.

EDDIE. That's what he likes to think. But I can read him.

PHEBE. What was his crime?

EDDIE. Uh?

PHEBE. If you can read him, then you will know his crime.

EDDIE. There is only ever one crime: theft.

PHEBE. You are simple.

EDDIE. Many degrees of it, but only one crime.

PHEBE. Clever but simple.

EDDIE. The thief of property is your common thief. The thief
of the person is called your aggravator. The thief of ideas is
your political prisoner. It is all theft at any rate.

PHEBE. Mr Mystery is none of those. You cannot read him.

EDDIE. His crime doesn't matter. What matters is: will he keep
dumb? I say he is no squealer.

PHEBE. I say so too.

EDDIE. He is a strong man, and that is what we need in a
mutiny.

PHEBE. Do not say that word.

EDDIE. Mutiny. That is what we are planning.

PHEBE. It is not a word I like to hear at sea.

EDDIE. Sea is where you are most like to hear it. Go through the cast. William will not join, if his play is a success, it will mark him out as a better class of convict in the colony so he has too much to lose. The Johnny Raw would squeal to the captain.

PHEBE. The vicar –

EDDIE. Don't jest.

PHEBE. There's a desperate fellow –

EDDIE. So it is Ben the forger or Mr Mystery. The knowable man or the unknowable man.

PHEBE. Forgers give themselves airs. There is more of the law about them than the criminal.

EDDIE. But they are dependable. There is no mystery about them.

PHEBE. All right.

EDDIE. You are agreed?

PHEBE. Yes. Tell him. Here he comes.

EDDIE. You think so?

PHEBE. I said it once. I think so.

BEN *comes on*.

EDDIE. I have decided on a liking for you.

BEN. Careful.

EDDIE. Careful is ever your watchword. That I respect.

BEN. There is no room on this ship for carelessness. Or for likings.

EDDIE. That is why I am going to tell you my plan.

BEN. Tell me nothing.

EDDIE. A group of us will seize the vessel and make her our own. Will you be among that number or will you remain a slave for the rest of your days?

BEN *looks around warily.*

BEN. Seize the vessel.

EDDIE. Yes.

BEN. And what then?

EDDIE. We sail her to America.

BEN. And what then?

EDDIE. America is the land of the free. Once there we are made.

BEN. How so?

EDDIE. Their Senate will reward us. It is their written policy.
    They were rebels against the British Crown. So will we be.
    They will give each one of us four acres of land. Our own land.

BEN. Four acres?

EDDIE. God's truth. I read it in a letter.

BEN. What letter?

EDDIE. Someone else's. While we were on the hulk. He kept it
    in a pocket. It was his hope.

BEN. The dreams of men on hulks –

EDDIE. Do you say it is not true?

BEN. We capture the ship.

EDDIE. Break open the arms chest. Four good men and true
    can hold up the whole ship's company. Get the discontents
    on our side, overboard with the captain and officers, change
    course and set sail for freedom.

BEN. You think that is possible?

EDDIE. Imagine the life we are sailing to.

BEN. I can. I do. But I love my own skin.

EDDIE. What are you saying?

BEN. Capture the ship. Capture the ship? Firstly you must gain
    the arms chest which is always heavily guarded.

EDDIE. There are lax moments –

BEN. Secondly you must break into the arms chest which is locked –

EDDIE. A heavy hammer and a strong arm –

BEN. Thirdly, you must pray the pistols are primed, powdered and ready and that the sea has not rusted their mechanisms –

EDDIE. They are discharged daily –

BEN. Fourthly you must be prepared to stand fast against the crew's cutlasses –

EDDIE. Powder against steel, I know where my money sits –

BEN. Fifthly you must inspire confidence in the prisoners. They must believe that a rebel life with you as leader is better than what they have –

EDDIE. It could not be worse –

BEN. Sixthly you must steer an accurate course past hostile shipping to a place you have never been with no officers and a crew of pressed men. Finally you arrive on an unknown shore, demand audience of the local power and say: 'Here be two hundred of us desperate creatures, give us four acres of land apiece,' as was written in a forgotten letter in the sodden pocket of Colin Cut-throat, Prince o' the Hulks.

EDDIE. Yes.

BEN. It is the most desperate scheme I ever heard.

EDDIE. Yes.

Pause.

BEN. I am with you. Not because of your plan which is a gallon of dirty bilge water, but because of your spirit.

EDDIE. You are with me?

BEN. I have at long last met a man more desperate than myself. When do we spring?

EDDIE. On leaving Rio. The boat will be fit, we hug the coast and head north.

PHEBE. Company!

EDDIE. More of this later.

EDDIE disappears. The rest of the COMPANY *troop on.*

WILLIAM. Friends. Friends all. Spirits have been low of late. Believe me, this is a common experience in a play, any play. We begin in a mood of excitement. As we approach the end, a delicious kind of fear envelops us. But the middle, ah the middle. We lose our way. We become dissatisfied with what we have done. We quarrel among ourselves. The voyage seems unending. And with our other difficulties, this mood is doubly hard to endure. But we must go on. We must help each other lift our spirits.

This pep talk seems to depress almost everybody. Suddenly:

TOM. Not me.

WILLIAM. What?

TOM. Not me. This is the best of all. This is the best of all that ever I did.

One or two looks from the COMPANY.

It was hard. 'Cos I can't read. I must have it all read to me. And then I must hold it in my head. Sometimes my head wants to burst. But I can do it. By the Lord, Harry, I can do it. And when I do it, I am not on the ship. (*Pause.*) Obviously I am on the ship. But in my head I am somewhere else. So my spirits is not low.

Everyone is moved. WILLIAM *goes over to* TOM. *He looks at him, not quite knowing how to applaud his speech. Eventually he thumps him on the shoulder.* TOM *grins.*

BETT. Come on, everyone. You all heard that.

Everyone is galvanised.

WILLIAM. Well spoken. Well spoken. Let's do one of the big company scenes.

But as the COMPANY *head for their places,* MAC-NAUGHTON *comes on.*

MACNAUGHTON. So, Mr Vaughan. You are the captain of the ship theatrical just as I am the captain of the ship nautical. How goes your voyage?

WILLIAM. Much as does yours, Captain. We are, as it were, approaching Rio, which is to say, we are a third of the way through our work.

MACNAUGHTON. But I am sailing round half the world. You are putting on an entertainment. I had thought to have enjoyed already the fruits of your labours.

WILLIAM. You command a crew of professional sailors. My company are fine fellows all, but amateurs. They slip on the planking, they set their course awry and the rigging slips through their hands. Had I a crew who could shin up a sixty-foot wall of blank verse, I would have given you the complete works of Shakespeare by now.

MACNAUGHTON. Even so. Now that we are approaching Rio I am taking stock of the ship and its contents and I will take stock of you too. You are as hard to nail down as a trout to a mast. You will perform for me, my play captain, tomorrow night. An excerpt for myself and the Rio harbour master.

General consternation.

WILLIAM. My players do not have their parts perfectly, Captain.

MACNAUGHTON. But the harbour master speaks no English and I revel in the errors of others. So you will find us an easy audience to please. Six sharp.

MACNAUGHTON *goes.*

WILLIAM. Well. You heard him.

AMELIA. It's not possible.

EDDIE. If we're told to do it, it's possible. Chains and gun-powder and the lash make it possible.

HARRY. No. We must not think that way. We will perform, not because we are commanded, but because it will make us free. The captain seeks to torment us, by showing our inadequacies.

We will throw his cruelty back in his face. We will act, not like slaves but like people given a glimpse of freedom.

WILLIAM. There. There is your example.

BETT *comes forward*.

BETT. Rio. We nosed into the middle harbour. On every side there was children in rowing boats selling fruit. Pink, brown, black, all colours of children, all colours of fruit. We got to the inner harbour and, because England is their ally, they give us an eleven-gun salute. The boat shook so hard, four of our girls went into labour straight off. I had been midwifing like a thing possessed when aboard comes the harbour master and we was on.

The Rio preview begins. The COMPANY *have rudimentary costumes and props.*

Scene Eleven

LOCKIT, LUCY.

LOCKIT. Whence come you, Hussy?

LUCY. My Tears might answer that Question.

LOCKIT. You have then been whimpering and fondling, like a Spaniel, over that Fellow that hath abus'd you.

LUCY. One can't help Love; one can't cure it.

LOCKIT. Learn to bear your Husband's Death like a reasonable Woman. 'Tis not the fashion now-a-days, so much as to affect Sorrow upon these Occasions. Act like a Woman of Spirit, Hussy, and thank your Father for what he is doing.

AIR XXXI – *Of a noble race was Shenkin*.

LUCY.
    Is then his fate decreed, Sir?
    Such a Man can I think of quitting?

When first we met, so moves me yet,
See how my heart is splitting!

LOCKIT. Look ye, Lucy – there is no saving him – so, I think,
you must ev'n do like other widows – buy yourself weeds,
and be cheerful.

AIR XXXII – *You'll think ere many days ensue.*

You'll think ere many Days ensue
This Sentence not severe;
I hang your Husband, Child, 'tis true,
But with him hang your Care.
Twang dang dillo dee.

You can't have the Man. So get all the money you can from
him.

Scene Twelve

LUCY, MACHEATH.

LUCY. The Ordinary was out of the way to-day. But I hope you
will upon the first Opportunity quiet my Scruples. Oh Sir!
my Father's heart is not to be soften'd, and I am in the
utmost Despair.

MACHEATH. Would not twenty Guineas, think you, move
him? Of all the Arguments in the way of Business, the most
prevailing is the Perquisite. Your Father's Perquisites for the
Escape of Prisoners must amount to a considerable Sum in
the Year. Money properly apply'd, will do anything.

LUCY. What Love or Money can do shall be done: for all my
Comfort depends upon your Safety.

Scene Thirteen

LUCY, MACHEATH, POLLY.

POLLY. Where is my dear Husband? Was a Rope ever intended for this Neck! O let me throw my Arms about it, and throttle thee with Love! Why dost thou turn away from me? 'Tis thy Polly. 'Tis thy Wife.

MACHEATH. Was there ever such an unfortunate Rascal as I am!

LUCY. Was there ever such another Villain!

POLLY. O MacHeath! was it for this we parted? Taken! Imprison'd! Try'd! Hang'd! I'll stay with thee till Death. What means my Love? Not one kind Word! not one kind Look! think what thy Polly suffers to see thee in this Condition.

SONG.– *'Only You' by Elvis Presley.*

MACHEATH. I must disown her. (*Aside.*) The wench is distracted.

LUCY. Am I then bilk'd of my Virtue? Sure Men were born to lie, and Women to believe them!

POLLY. Am I not thy Wife? Look at me. Tell me, am I not thy Wife?

LUCY. Perfidious Wretch!

POLLY. Barbarous Husband!

LUCY. Hadst thou been hang'd five Months ago, I had been happy.

POLLY. And I too. You swore to be kind to me till Death us parted! And that's no unreasonable Request to a Man who hath not seven Days to live.

LUCY. Hast thou two Wives, Monster?

MACHEATH. If you can cease for an answer, hear me.

LUCY. I won't. Flesh and Blood can't bear my Usage.

POLLY. Shall I not claim my own? Justice bids me speak.

AIR XXXV – *Have you heard of a frolicsome ditty, etc.*

MACHEATH.
> How happy could I be with either,
> Were t'other dear Charmer away!
> But while you thus teaze me together,
> To neither a Word will I say;
> But tol de rol (*etc.*)

POLLY. He must be distracted with his Misfortunes, or he could not use me thus.

LUCY. O Villain, Villain! Thou hast deceiv'd me. I could inform against thee with Pleasure.

AIR XXXVI – *Irish Trot.*

POLLY.
> I am bubbled.

LUCY.
> I'm bubbled.

POLLY.
> O how I am troubled!

LUCY.
> Bamboozled, and bit!

POLLY.
> My Distresses are doubled.

LUCY.
> When you come to the Tree,
> Should the Hangman refuse,
> These Fingers, with Pleasure,
> Could fasten the Noose.

POLLY.
> I'm bubbled (*etc.*)

MACHEATH. Be pacified, my dear Lucy. This is all a Fetch of Polly's to make me desperate with you in case I get off. If I am to be hang'd, she would fain have the Credit of being thought my Widow. Really, Polly, this is no time for a

Dispute of this sort. You may be talking of Marriage, but I am thinking of Hanging.

POLLY. And hast thou the Heart to disown me?

MACHEATH. And hast thou the Heart to persuade me that I am married? Why, Polly, dost thou seek to aggravate my Misfortunes?

LUCY. Really, Miss Peachum, you but expose yourself. Besides, 'tis barbarous in you to worry a Gentleman in his Circumstances.

AIR XXXVII

POLLY.
>Cease your Funning;
>Force or Cunning
>Never shall my Heart trepan.
>All these Sallies are but Malice
>To seduce my constant Man.
>'Tis most certain, By their flirting
>Women oft have Envy shown
>Pleas'd to ruin Others wooing;
>Never happy in their own!

LUCY. Decency, Madam, methinks might teach you to behave yourself with some Reserve with the Husband, while his Wife is present.

MACHEATH. But seriously, Polly, this is carrying the Joke a little too far.

LUCY. If you are determin'd, Madam, to raise a Disturbance in the Prison, I shall be oblig'd to send for the Turnkey to shew you the Door.

POLLY. Give me leave to tell you, Madam: these forward Airs don't become you in the least, Madam. And my Duty, Madam, obliges me to stay with my Husband, Madam.

AIR XXXVIII – *Good-morrow, gossip Joan.*

LUCY.
>Why how now, Madam Flirt?
>If you thus must chatter;

> And are for flinging Dirt,
> Let's see who best can spatter;
> Madam Flirt!

POLLY.

> Why how now, saucy Jade;
> Sure the Wench is tipsy!
> How can you see me made
> (*To* MACHEATH.) The scoff of such a Gipsy?
> (*To* LUCY.) Saucy Jade!

Scene Fourteen

LUCY, MACHEATH, POLLY, PEACHUM.

PEACHUM. Where's my Wench? Ah, Hussy! Hussy! Come you home, you Slut; and when your Fellow is hang'd, hang yourself, to make your Family some Amends.

POLLY. Dear, dear Father, do not tear me from him. I have more to say. Oh! twist thy Fetters about me, that he may not haul me from thee!

PEACHUM. Not a Word more! You are my Prisoner now, Hussy.

SONG – '*Stand By Me*' *by Ben E. King*.

> POLLY *sings, holding* MACHEATH, *as* PEACHUM *pulls her.*

Scene Fifteen

LUCY, MACHEATH.

MACHEATH. I am naturally Compassionate, Wife; so I could not use the Wench as she deserv'd; which made you at first suspect there was something in what she said.

LUCY. Indeed, my Dear, I was strangely puzzled.

MACHEATH. If that had been the Case, her Father would never have brought me into this Circumstance. No, Lucy, I had rather die than be false to thee.

LUCY. How happy I am, if you say this from your heart! For I love thee so, that I could sooner bear to see thee hang'd than in the Arms of another.

MACHEATH. You see, Lucy; in the account of Love you are in my debt, and you must now be convinc'd, that I rather choose to die than be another's. Make me, if possible, love thee more, and let me owe my Life to thee. If you refuse to assist me, Peachum and your Father will immediately put me beyond all means of Escape.

LUCY. My Father hath been drinking hard with the Prisoners and is now taking his Nap. See I have procured the Key.

She holds it up. MACHEATH *takes it.*

Shall I go off with thee, my Dear?

MACHEATH. T'will be impossible for both of us to lie conceal'd. As soon as the Search cools, I will send to thee. Till then my Heart is thy Prisoner.

LUCY. Come then, my dear Husband, owe thy life to me: But that Polly runs in my Head strangely.

MACHEATH. Hurry! A moment of Time may make us unhappy for ever.

MACHEATH *edges away to the side of the stage.*

AIR XL – *The lass of Patie's mill, etc.*

LUCY.
> I like the Fox shall grieve,
> Whose Mate hath left her Side,
> Whom Hounds from Morn to Eve,
> Chase o'er the Country wide.
> Where can my Lover hide?
> Where cheat the weary Pack?
> If love be not his Guide,
> He never will come back!

The performance ends. MACNAUGHTON *stares at* LUCY. *He has fallen in love with her.*

MACNAUGHTON. Excellent. (*Holding it in.*) A very pert Lucy.

LUCY. Thank you, Captain.

MACNAUGHTON (*losing it*). What a beautiful flower to discover in such a benighted wood.

LUCY. Thank you, Captain.

MACNAUGHTON. But your leading man, where is he, the villainous MacHeath?

All look around. No HARRY. *A* SAILOR *runs on.*

SAILOR. Captain! He's gone over the side. While we was all watching. Took his irons off with that key! He's in Rio!

MACNAUGHTON *and the* SAILOR *rush out. The* COMPANY *look at each other. They have been betrayed.*

ACT THREE

Scene One

Newgate. LOCKIT, LUCY.

LOCKIT. To be sure, Wench, you must have been aiding and abetting him to help him to this Escape.

LUCY. Sir, here hath been Peachum and his Daughter Polly, and to be sure they know the Ways of Newgate as well as if they had been born and bred in the Place all their Lives. Why must all your Suspicion light upon me?

LOCKIT. I will have none of these shuffling answers.

LUCY. If I know anything of MacHeath I wish I may be burnt!

LOCKIT. Did he tip handsomely? Come, Hussy, don't cheat your Father; and I shall not be angry with you. Perhaps, you

have made a better Bargain with him than I could have done.
How much, my good Girl?

LUCY. You know, Sir, I am fond of him, and would have given
him money to have kept him with me.

LOCKIT. Ah Lucy! thy Education might have put thee more
upon thy Guard.

LUCY. Dear Sir, mention not my Education for 'twas to that I
owe my Ruin.

AIR XLI – *If love's a sweet passion, etc.*

When young at the Bar you first taught me to score,
And bid me be free of my Lips and no more;
I was kissed by the Parson, the Squire, and the Sot
When the guest was departed the Kiss was forgot.
But his Kiss was so sweet, and so closely he prest,
That I languish'd and pin'd till I granted the rest.

If you can forgive me, Sir, I will make a fair Confession, for
to be sure he hath been a most barbarous Villain to me.

LOCKIT. And so you have let him escape, Hussy, have you?

LUCY. When a Woman loves, a kind Look, a tender Word
can persuade her to anything – and I could ask no other
Bribe.

LOCKIT. Thou wilt always be a vulgar Slut, Lucy. You should
never do anything but upon the foot of Interest.

LUCY. But Love, Sir, is a Misfortune that may happen to the
most discreet Woman, and in Love we are all Fools alike.

SONG – *'Only Love Can Break Your Heart' by Neil Young.*

Notwithstanding all that he swore, I am now fully convinc'd
that Polly Peachum is actually his Wife. And I let him escape
to go to her. Polly will wheedle herself into his Money, and
then Peachum will hang him, and cheat us both.

LOCKIT. And so I am to be ruin'd, because you are in Love!

LUCY. I could murder that impudent Strumpet.

LOCKIT. And so, after all this Mischief, I must stay here to be entertain'd with your Catterwauling, Mistress Puss! Out of my Sight, wanton Strumpet! you shall fast and mortify yourself into Reason. Go!

Scene Two

LOCKIT. Peachum then intends to outwit me in this Affair; but I'll be even with him. The Dog is leaky in his Liquor, so I'll ply him that way, get the Secret from him, and turn this Affair to my own Advantage. Lions, Wolves and Vultures don't live together in Herds, Droves, or Flocks. Of all Animals of Prey, Man is the only sociable one. Every one of us preys upon the other, and yet we herd together. Peachum is my Companion, my Friend. According to the Custom of the World, indeed he may quote thousands of Precedents for Cheating me. And shall I not make use of the Privilege of Friendship to make him a Return?

SONG – *'Ain't No Cure for Love' by Leonard Cohen*.

A Gamester's a hungry pike: they will work together to secure the destruction of a third. But when the prey slips away, they turn upon each other.

Lucy!

Enter LUCY.

Are there any of Peachum's People now in the House?

LUCY. Filch, Sir, is drinking a Quartern of Strong-Waters in the next Room with Black Moll.

LOCKIT. Bid him come to me.

Suddenly HARRY *is there. He looks grim. The* COMPANY *stare at him. Eventually:*

BETT. Why d'you do it, Harry?

HARRY. I'm sorry.

GRACE. We trusted you. You inspired us all. 'We will act, not like slaves but like people given a glimpse of freedom.'

BEN. He had his glimpse of freedom. Didn't you, tosspot? Half an hour. Nice glimpse, was it?

HARRY. I wasn't lying to you. That's exactly what happened.

BETT. What d'you mean?

HARRY. In my mind. I became him.

BETT. Who?

HARRY. MacHeath.

BEN. Oh my good Christ.

HARRY. A hero. Someone bigger than you ever find in life. A man who could laugh at captivity, even laugh at death. I was playing him, and then I wanted to be him, and then I was him. I didn't think about it. I was him.

WILLIAM. You played the hero. At everyone else's expense.

PHEBE. I don't mind that, I mind that you used us as cover.

BEN. I don't mind that. I mind that you got caught.

HARRY. Hundred lashes. Two weeks' solitary.

AMELIA. Deserved it.

WILLIAM. You were lucky. I thought he would hang you.

BEN. Seen it done. I've seen 'em choked for less.

AMELIA. The wry face and the wet breech.

GRACE. So why are you here, actually? We're busy with a rehearsal.

HARRY. Captain thought... Captain thought. Maybe I was needed.

Pause.

GRACE. Don't need you, Harry. After what you done.

Pause.

BARTLEMY. Of course we need him. We've struggled on. Everyone has tried hard. But there's no spark. Harry has the voice, the voice that lifts the soul!

Everyone is amazed at BARTLEMY's *intervention.*

GRACE. Shut up. You're a vicar.

BEN. Man's entitled, man's entitled.

GRACE. If he's a vicar he has to shut up.

BEN. Man's entitled.

TOM. No one else can play MacHeath.

EDDIE. Thank you very much.

TOM. Captain took a look at last rehearsal. I reckon he's ready to close us down.

GRACE. I'm not working with him.

EDDIE. Well, I will.

BEN. Oh fuck, I can feel another vote coming on.

PHEBE. What did the captain say to you?

HARRY. The captain is a first-time captain. He has no experience so he is ruled by his whims. His whim is that I shall return and the play will continue.

Pause as this sinks in.

EDDIE. Ben. You need not fear. There will be no vote.

HARRY (*to* WILLIAM). You called me Mr Mystery. But I am none such. My first crime was stealing. Fourteen years old. A desperate raid on a vegetable garden to feed my brothers and sisters. Seven years transportation for a handful of cauliflowers. I thought I had known the meaning of hunger. But then came the first winter in Australia. Even the soldiers went hungry, even the Governor. I kept my head down and survived, a boy among men. And I was changed.

A snigger from someone.

Not in the way you think. I was purified. On the ship back I had one thought: now that I have been cleansed they cannot touch me. But they had a different opinion. I was a convict. So when our rich farmer gets his throat cut and his gold taken, I must be the culprit, mustn't I? I made my escape in Rio because I was owed it.

GRACE. Funny, isn't it? The way everybody is innocent.

But some have been affected by HARRY's *story.*

WILLIAM. Act Three, Scene Three.

EDDIE *hands* HARRY *a script. Everyone accepts the situation in their own way. The rehearsal resumes.*

Scene Three

LOCKIT. FILCH *comes in, knackered.*

LOCKIT. Why, Boy, thou lookest as if thou wert half starv'd, like a shotten Herring.

FILCH. One had need have the Constitution of a Horse to go through with the Business. Who wrote the law that a pregnant woman cannot hang? I have pick'd up a little Money this morning by attempting to bring four Ladies into a state where the gallows cannot claim them. But if a Man cannot get an honest Livelihood any easier way, I am a cabbage.

LOCKIT. Boy, it is noble work you do, and you shall find rest in Heaven. But canst thou tell me where thy Master is to be found?

FILCH. At his Lock, Sir, at the Crooked Billet.

LOCKIT. I'll go to him there. We'll walk together.

FILCH *shakes his head.*

Lean on me and we'll walk together.

FILCH *shakes his head.* LOCKIT *picks him up and carries him.*

Scene Four

A gaming house. MACHEATH, *in a fine tarnished coat,* BEN BUDGE, MATT OF THE MINT.

MACHEATH. I am sorry the Road was so barren of Money. (*Gives them money.*) See, Gentlemen, I am not a mere Court Friend, who professes every thing and will do nothing.

AIR XLIV – *Lillibullero.*

> The Modes of the Court so common are grown,
> That a true Friend can hardly be met;
> Friendship for Interest is but a Loan,
> Which they let out for what they can get,
> 'Tis true, you find Some Friends so kind,
> Who will give you good Counsel themselves to defend.
> In sorrowful Ditty, they promise, they pity,
> But shift you for Money, from Friend to Friend.

BUDGE. It grieves my Heart that so generous a Man as you should be obliged to live with such ill Company, and herd with Gamesters.

MATT. See the Partiality of Mankind! One man may steal a Horse, better than another may look over a Hedge. Of all servile handicrafts-men, a Gamester is the vilest. But yet, as many of the Quality are of the Profession, he is admitted among the politest Company. I wonder we are not more respected.

MACHEATH. There will be deep Play to-night at Mary-bone, and consequently Money may be pick'd up upon the Road. Meet me there, and I'll give you the Hint who is worth Setting.

BUDGE. At Mary-bone.

MACHEATH. Your servant, gentlemen.

Scene Five

PEACHUM*'s lock. A table with wine, brandy, pipes, and tobacco.*

LOCKIT. The Coronation Account, Brother Peachum, is of so intricate a nature, that I believe it will never be settled. (*Reading ledger.*) A Lady's Tail of rich Brocade – that, I see, is dispos'd of.

PEACHUM. To Mrs Diana Trapes, the Tally-Woman.

LOCKIT. But I don't see any Article of the Jewels.

PEACHUM. Those are so well known that they must be sent abroad. You'll find them enter'd upon the Article of Exportation. As for the Snuff-Boxes, Watches, Swords, etc. I thought it best to enter them under their several Heads.

LOCKIT. Seven and twenty Women's Pockets complete; with the several things therein contain'd; all Seal'd, Number'd, and Enter'd.

PEACHUM. But, Brother, it is impossible for us now to enter upon all this accursed accounting. We should have the whole Day before us. Besides, the main ledger lies at the other Office.

LOCKIT. Bring us then more Liquor. To-day shall be for Pleasure, Tomorrow for Business. Ah, Brother, those Daughters of ours are two slippery Hussies. Keep a watchful eye upon Polly, and MacHeath in a day or two shall be our own again.

AIR XLV – *Down in the north country, etc.*

> What Gudgeons are we Men!
> Ev'ry Woman's easy Prey.
> Though we have felt the Hook, again
> We bite and they betray.
> The Bird that hath been trapt,
> When he hears his calling Mate,
> To her he flies, again he's clapt
> Within the wiry Grate.

PEACHUM. But what signifies catching the Bird, if your
Daughter Lucy will set open the Door of the Cage?

LOCKIT. This is unkind of you, Brother. If Men were answerable for the Follies and Frailties of the Wives and Daughters,
no Friends could keep a good Correspondence together for
two Days.

Enter a SERVANT.

SERVANT. Sir, here's Mrs Diana Trapes wants to speak with you.

PEACHUM. Shall we admit her, Brother Lockit?

LOCKIT. By all means, She's a good Customer, and a fine-
spoken Woman. And a Woman who drinks and talks so
freely, will enliven the Conversation.

PEACHUM. Desire her to walk in.

Exit SERVANT. *The* COMPANY *look at* WILLIAM.

WILLIAM. Good. I have only three points there: pace, pace
and pace.

Lights change. Night-time. BARTLEMY *and* AMELIA.
BARTLEMY *is animated.*

AMELIA. Reverend Wilkins. Are you quite well?

BARTLEMY. Amelia. I am more than well. I have begun to
enjoy it!

AMELIA. The play?

BARTLEMY. I have always performed alone before. Standing
in a joyless pulpit, preaching down to wandering minds.
Now I am standing shoulder to shoulder with my fellows for
the first time. I depend on them, they depend on me. It is an
epiphany. Here we are, sailing into Cape Town and I realise
for the first time I am linked to humanity.

AMELIA. Reverend Wilkins. Would you like to be linked a
little more?

She grabs him and pulls him into the shadows. PHEBE,
EDDIE *and* WILLIAM *appear.*

PHEBE. Well?

EDDIE. Always the accuser.

PHEBE. That's the position you put me in.

BEN. We couldn't do it in Rio. Once Harry went over the side you couldn't scratch your arse without a guard flashing his cutlass.

PHEBE. Rio was a month ago. This is Cape Town and it's the last stop. The chance will not come again.

EDDIE. We're here for a week.

PHEBE. We might be here for a week. With this captain, he could up anchor and sail if he doesn't like the look of the harbour master's parrot. It must be tonight.

BEN. Tonight? Tonight don't feel right.

PHEBE. What feels wrong?

BEN. Just something.

EDDIE. He's right.

PHEBE. Something in the air?

BEN. If you like.

PHEBE *turns away.*

EDDIE. What?

PHEBE. Three hundred men on the boat. I have to pick the two with lily livers.

EDDIE. Oh no, oh no, you can't pin that on me.

PHEBE. Then prove me wrong.

EDDIE. Why am I on this boat?

PHEBE. You drank a skinful of moonshine and threw a stone at a redcoat.

EDDIE. I led a rebellion!

PHEBE. They'd have hanged you for that, ye gobshite.

EDDIE. There was a dozen of us with pikes and we stormed the guardhouse at Tuam.

BEN. Eh? You did what?

PHEBE. A wonderful thing is the imagination.

BEN. I didn't know about this.

PHEBE. It doesn't matter. Storm the arms chest? Hoist the captain over the side? You two wouldn't steal a biscuit from the ship's doctor.

BEN. Events have not been what they might.

PHEBE. Oh, 'events'.

BEN. There is not the discontent I expected. This captain is changeable but he's not a tyrant. The surgeon is a good man.

PHEBE. And because of these 'events', I will now endure a life of slavery on a foreign shore.

EDDIE (*to* PHEBE). It will not be so bad, the two of us together.

PHEBE. It will not be the two of us together. Unless you take your hand to the arms chest, I will not let you inside me again.

A moment. EDDIE is on the verge of going for it. He looks at BEN. But BEN looks away. PHEBE knows the moment has passed.

Men! I have fallen in love with them and it does not help. I have tried to use them for their valour and it does not help. Nothing with men helps!

Suddenly MACNAUGHTON is there.

MACNAUGHTON. A common complaint I understand. But what occasions the remark tonight?

MACNAUGHTON is close to EDDIE.

Eh?

EDDIE. I don't have to say nothing.

MACNAUGHTON. That's an opinion.

EDDIE. Even on a convict ship there is privacy between man and woman.

MACNAUGHTON. Is there now? Is this a rehearsal?

PHEBE. It will be.

And, indeed, the COMPANY *gradually appear in ones and twos until everyone is present.*

MACNAUGHTON. Well, if it be a rehearsal, I surely have some jurisdiction over it. And I demand that you, Eddie Cosgrove, tell me of what you were speaking. After all, you may have been speaking of mutiny.

WILLIAM. Captain. I think we may be sufficiently trusted –

MACNAUGHTON. After what happened in Rio, that is impossible. Cosgrove. Step forward.

BETT. I am Eddie Cosgrove!

Pause. MACNAUGHTON *turns to* BETT, *not quite understanding.*

TOM. And I am Eddie Cosgrove.

AMELIA. And I am Eddie Cosgrove.

Gradually, all the COMPANY *repeat the formula as they stand up to* MACNAUGHTON. *Some moments.*

MACNAUGHTON. Well. It seems you are all present. Carry on with your rehearsal.

MACNAUGHTON *goes.*

EDDIE. Thank you. Everyone.

GRACE. Captain was right.

TOM. What?

GRACE. There was a kind of mutiny.

WILLIAM. A small one. Now. To your places. Act Three, Scene Six.

Scene Six

PEACHUM, LOCKIT, MRS TRAPES.

PEACHUM. Dear Mrs Dye, your Servant. One may know by
your Kiss, that your Ginn is excellent.

TRAPES. I was always very curious in my Liquors.

LOCKIT. There is no perfum'd Breath like it. I have been long
acquainted with the Flavour of those Lips. Han't I, Mrs Dye?

TRAPES. Fill it up! I take as large Draughts of Liquor, as I did
of Love. I hate a Flincher in either.

SONG – *to the tune of 'Those Were the Days' by Gene Raskin
and Mary Hopkin*.

> When I was young I practised osculation
> I wet my lips and kissed till they were sore
> My mouth went places way above its station
> And many well below you may be sure.
>
> Those were the days, my friend
> We thought they'd never end
> We'd sing and dance for ever and a day
> We'd live the life we'd choose
> We'd fornicate and booze
> Those were the days, oh yes those were the days!
>
> But nowadays my mouth's more used to swigging
> I guzzle down Madeira, gin and grog
> So though I'm not so occupied with frigging
> You'll be off your face when I give you a snog.
>
> But now, Mr Peachum, to our Business. If you have Blacks
> of any kind, brought in of late; Mantoes, Velvet Scarfs, Petti-
> coats – let it be what it will, I am your Chap, for all my
> Ladies are very fond of Mourning.

PEACHUM. Why, look ye, Mrs Dye. You deal so hard with us,
that we can afford to give only a pittance to the Gentlemen,
who venture their Lives for the Goods.

TRAPES. The hard Times oblige me to go very near in my Dealing. And, o' my Conscience, now-a-days most Ladies take a Delight in cheating, when they can do it with Safety.

PEACHUM. Madam, you have had a handsome Gold Watch of us t'other Day for seven Guineas. Considering we must have our Profit, to a Gentleman upon the Road, a Gold Watch will be scarce worth the taking.

TRAPES. Consider, Mr Peachum, that Watch was remarkable, and not of very safe Sale. If you have any black Velvet Scarfs, they are a handsome Winter-wear, and take with most Gentlemen who deal with my Customers. 'Tis I that put the Ladies of the Town upon a good Foot. 'Tis not Youth or Beauty that fixes their Price, oh no. The Gentlemen always pay according to their Dress, from half a Crown to two Guineas; and yet those Hussies are for ever bilking me. And what with Fees and other Expenses, there are great Goings-out and no Comings in. We run great Risks, great Risks indeed.

PEACHUM. As I remember, you said something just now of Mrs Coaxer.

TRAPES. Yes, Sir. To be sure I stript her of a Suit of my own Clothes about two Hours ago; and have left her as she should be, in her Shift, with a Lover of hers at my House. She call'd him up Stairs, as he was going to Mary-bone in a Hackney Coach. And I hope, for her own sake and mine, she will per-suade the Captain to redeem her, for the Captain is very gen-erous to the Ladies.

LOCKIT. What Captain?

TRAPES. An intimate Acquaintance of yours, Mr Peachum – only Captain MacHeath – as fine as a Lord.

PEACHUM. Tomorrow, Mrs Dye, you shall set your own Price upon any of the Goods you like. We have at least half a Dozen Velvet Scarfs, and all at your Service. Will you give me leave to make you a Present of the Suit of Night-clothes for your own wearing? But are you sure it is Captain MacHeath?

TRAPES. Nobody knows him better. I have taken a great deal of the Captain's Money in my Time at second-hand, for he always lov'd to have his ladies well drest.

PEACHUM. Mr Lockit and I have a little Business with the Captain, you understand me, and we will satisfy you for Mrs Coaxer's Debt.

LOCKIT. Depend upon it. We will deal like Men of Honour.

TRAPES. I don't enquire after your Affairs, so whatever happens, I wash my hands on't. It hath always been my Maxim, that one Friend should assist another. But if you please, I'll take one of the Scarfs home with me. 'Tis always good to have something in Hand.

A moment backstage. Amidst confusion and costume changes, AMELIA *finds a moment with* BARTLEMY.

AMELIA. Reverend Wilkins. I must speak with you.

BARTLEMY. In the middle of a performance?

AMELIA. The moment of weakness that passed between us, that night before Cape Town –

BARTLEMY. Please, do not speak of it. I have prayed for both of us. There is a stain on my soul and it will not come out.

AMELIA. Never mind your soul. I am with child. Your child. What am I to do?

BARTLEMY. I –

AMELIA. You prayed for my soul and delivered me from evil. But in the end it was you who brought me to temptation.

BARTLEMY. I am respectable. I have a respectable future, a parish and a harpsichord.

AMELIA. And I had nothing, and now have less. Excuse me, I must reserve my passion for the stage.

She brushes past him to appear as LUCY.

Scene Seven

Newgate. LUCY.

LUCY. Jealousy, Rage, Love and Fear are at once tearing me to pieces. How am I weather-beaten and shatter'd with Distresses! While I lie awake at night, Polly rolls in voluptuous pleasure! Revenge, revenge, revenge shall appease my restless spirit.

I have the Rats-bane ready. I run no Risk; for I can lay her Death upon the Ginn, and so many die of that I shall never be call'd in question.

Enter FILCH.

FILCH. Madam, here's Miss Polly come to wait upon you.

LUCY. Show her in.

Scene Eight

LUCY, POLLY.

LUCY. Dear Madam, your Servant. I hope you will pardon my Passion, when I was so happy to see you last. I was so over-run with the Spleen, that I was perfectly out of myself. I earnestly wish all our Quarrels might have a comfortable Reconciliation.

POLLY. I have no Excuse for my own Behaviour, Madam, but my Misfortunes.

LUCY. But, Miss Polly – in the way of Friendship, will you give me leave to propose a Glass of cordial to you?

POLLY. Strong-Waters are apt to give me the Head-Ache. I hope, Madam, you will excuse me.

LUCY. Not the greatest Lady in the Land could have better in her Closet, for her own private drinking.

POLLY. I am sorry, Madam, my Health will not allow me to accept of your Offer. I should not have left you in the rude manner I did when we met last, Madam. But really, the Captain treated me with so much Contempt and Cruelty, that I deserv'd your Pity, rather than your Resentment.

LUCY. But since his Escape, no doubt all Matters are made up again. Ah Polly! Polly! 'tis I am the unhappy Wife; and he loves you as if you were only his Mistress.

POLLY. Sure, Madam, you cannot think me so happy as to be the object of your Jealousy. A Man is always afraid of a Woman who loves him too well – so that I must expect to be neglected and avoided.

LUCY. Then our Cases, my dear Polly, are exactly alike. Both of us indeed have been too fond.

AIR XLIX – *O Bessy Bell*.

POLLY.
> A Curse attend that Woman's Love,
> Who always would be pleasing.

LUCY.
> The Pertness of the billing Dove,
> Like Tickling, is but teasing.

POLLY.
> What then in Love can Woman do;

LUCY.
> If we grow fond they shun us.

POLLY.
> And when we fly them, they pursue:

LUCY.
> But leave us when they've won us.

> Love is so very whimsical in both Sexes, that it is impossible to be lasting. But my Heart is particular, and contradicts my own Observation.

POLLY. But really, Mistress Lucy, by his last Behaviour, I think I ought to envy you. When I was forc'd from him, he did not shew the least Tenderness. But perhaps, he hath a Heart not capable of it.

SONG – *'Anyone Who Had a Heart' by Burt Bacharach and Hal David.*

The Coquettes of both Sexes are Self-lovers, and that is a Love no other whatever can dispossess. I hear, my dear Lucy, our Husband is one of those.

LUCY. Away with these melancholy Reflections, indeed, my dear Polly, we are both of us a Cup too low. Let me prevail upon you to accept of my Offer. Let's take a chirping Glass. Wine can clear the Vapours of Despair. I can't bear, Child, to see you in such low Spirits. And I must persuade you to what I know will do you good. (*Aside.*) I shall now soon be even with the hypocritical Strumpet.

An aside during the performance between AMELIA *and* GRACE.

GRACE. My dear Amelia, is your costume tight or are you carrying a little sailor amidships?

AMELIA. Hold your tongue, bitch.

GRACE. The little cherub will have a hundred fathers.

AMELIA. I have so loved this play with the one exception of having to spend time in your company.

GRACE. For my part, I have only been tempted to return to my arsonist past whenever I see you in your big, combustible frock.

AMELIA. Do have some of that drink, dear, the poison's practical.

GRACE. Get off the stage, lump, this is my big scene.

Scene Nine

POLLY. All this Wheedling of Lucy cannot be for nothing. At this time too, when I know she hates me! The Dissembling of a Woman is always the Forerunner of Mischief. By pouring Strong-Waters down my Throat, she thinks to pump some Secrets out of me. I'll be upon my Guard, and won't taste a Drop of her Liquor, I'm resolv'd.

Scene Ten

LUCY, *with strong waters*. POLLY.

LUCY. Come, Miss Polly.

POLLY. Indeed, Child, you have given yourself trouble to no purpose. You must, my Dear, excuse me.

LUCY. Really, Miss Polly, you are as squeamishly affected about taking a Cup of Strong-Waters as a Lady before Company. I vow, Polly, I shall take it monstrously ill if you refuse me.

POLLY. I protest, Madam, it goes against me.

She sees LOCKIT *and* PEACHUM *bringing in* MACHEATH *in chains.*

What do I see! MacHeath again in Custody! Now every Glimm'ring of Happiness is lost.

She drops the glass of liquor on the ground.

LUCY (*aside*). Since things are thus, I'm glad the Wench hath escap'd; for by this Event, 'tis plain, she was not happy enough to deserve to be poison'd.

Scene Eleven

LOCKIT, MACHEATH, PEACHUM, LUCY, POLLY.

LOCKIT. Captain, you have neither the Chance of Love or Money for another Escape, for you are order'd to be call'd down upon your Trial immediately.

PEACHUM. Away, Hussies! This is not a Time for a Man to be hamper'd with his Wives.

LUCY. O Husband, Husband, my Heart long'd to see thee; but to see thee thus distracts me.

POLLY. Will not my dear Husband look upon his Polly? Why had'st thou not flown to me for Protection?

AIR LII – *The last time I went o'er the moor.*

> Hither, dear Husband, turn your Eyes.

LUCY.
> Bestow one Glance to cheer me.

POLLY.
> Think with that Look, thy Polly dies.

LUCY.
> O shun me not, but hear me.

POLLY.
> 'Tis Polly sues.

LUCY.
> 'Tis Lucy speaks.

POLLY.
> Is thus true Love requited?

LUCY.
> My Heart is bursting.

POLLY.
> Mine too breaks.

LUCY.
> Must I –

POLLY.
    Must I be slighted?

MACHEATH. What would you have me say, Ladies? You see this Affair will soon be at an end, without my disobliging either of you.

PEACHUM. But the settling this Point, Captain, might prevent a Law-Suit between your two Widows.

MACHEATH. Which way shall I turn? On the Day of execution, a wife is as fond as a Bride. But two brides? No man can put up with that.

POLLY (*to* PEACHUM). Dear, dear Sir, sink the material Evidence, and bring him off at his Trial. Polly, upon her Knees begs it of you.

LUCY (*to* LOCKIT). If Peachum's Heart is harden'd; sure you, Sir, will have more Compassion on a Daughter. I know the Evidence is in your Power. How then can you be a Tyrant to me? (*Kneeling*.) O think of your Daughter, if I were his Wife, each month of my Life would hereafter be May.

LOCKIT. MacHeath's Time is come, Lucy. We know our own Affairs, therefore let us have no more Whimpering or Whining.

AIR LVI – *A cobbler there was, etc*.

    Ourselves, like the Great, to secure a Retreat,
    When Matters Require it, must give up our Gang:
    And good reason why, Or, instead of the Fry,
    Ev'n Peachum and I.
    Like poor petty Rascals, might hang, hang;
    Like poor petty Rascals, might hang.

PEACHUM. Set your Heart at rest, Polly. Your Husband is to die to-day. Therefore if you are not already provided, 'tis high time to look about for another. There's comfort for you, you Slut.

LOCKIT. We are ready, Sir, to conduct you to the Old Bailey.

MACHEATH. Here ends Dispute for th' remnant of our Lives,
    This way at least I should please both my Wives.

SONG – *'See That My Grave is Kept Clean' by Blind Lemon Jefferson.*

Now, Gentlemen, I am ready to attend you.

Scene Twelve

LUCY, POLLY, FILCH.

POLLY. Follow them, Filch, to the Court. And bring me an Account of his Behaviour.

Exit FILCH.

But why is all this Musick?

LUCY. The prisoners, whose Trials are put off till next Session, are diverting themselves.

A dance of PRISONERS *in chains to the tune of 'London Girls'. It's a wild restaging of the* PRISONERS' *rum dance. They clank their chains and metal cups while a* CONVICT *dressed as* MACNAUGHTON *doles out rum with a ladle.*

CONVICT (*as* MACNAUGHTON). Dance, ye devils, or you'll get no rum ration from me.

Scene Thirteen

The dance builds to a climax then cuts out, revealing MACHEATH, *alone in the condemned hold. He drinks.*

AIR LXVII – *Greensleeves.*

MACHEATH.
　　　Since Laws were made for ev'ry Degree,
　　　To curb Vice in others, as well as me,

I wonder we han't better Company,
Upon Tyburn Tree!
But Gold from Law can take out the Sting;
And if rich Men like us were to swing,
'Twould thin the Land, such Numbers to string
Upon Tyburn Tree!

JAILOR. Some Friends of yours, Captain, desire to be admitted. I leave you together.

Scene Fourteen

MACHEATH, BEN BUDGE, MATT OF THE MINT.

MACHEATH. For my having broke Prison, you see, Gentlemen, I am order'd immediate Execution.

MATT. We are heartily sorry, Captain, for your Misfortune – but 'tis what we must all come to.

MACHEATH. Peachum and Lockit, you know, are infamous Scoundrels. Remember your dying Friend! 'Tis my last Request. Bring those Villains to the Gallows before you, and I am satisfied.

MATT. We'll do it.

BUDGE. Miss Polly and Miss Lucy entreat a Word with you.

MACHEATH. Gentlemen, adieu.

A moment backstage as BARTLEMY *comes off and* AMELIA *comes on.*

BARTLEMY. I have considered. I shall do the honest thing. You shall be a vicar's wife in New South Wales.

AMELIA. Reverend Wilkins! We shall pray every day.

BARTLEMY. We shall!

WILLIAM. Amelia, get on!

WILLIAM *gives* BARTLEMY *an astonished look.*

Scene Fifteen

LUCY, MACHEATH, POLLY.

MACHEATH. My dear Lucy. My dear Polly. Whatsoever hath pass'd between us is now at an end. If you are fond of marrying again, the best Advice I can give you is to Ship yourselves to the West Indies, where you'll have a fair Chance of getting a Husband a-piece, or by good Luck, two or three, as you like best.

POLLY. How can I support this Sight!

LUCY. There is nothing moves one so much as a great Man in Distress. Would I might be hang'd!

POLLY. And I would so too! Will you leave me no Token of Love?

LUCY. Will you leave me no Token of Love?

MACHEATH. I hear the Toll of the Bell.

POLLY. Adieu.

LUCY. Farewell.

Scene Sixteen

To them, enter PLAYER *and* BEGGAR (JOHN GAY).

PLAYER. But, honest Friend, I hope you don't intend that MacHeath shall be really executed.

JOHN GAY. Most certainly, Sir. To make the Piece perfect, I was for doing strict poetical Justice – MacHeath is to be hang'd; and for the other Personages of the Drama, the Audience must have suppos'd they were all hang'd or transported.

PLAYER. Why then Friend, this is a downright deep Tragedy. The Catastrophe is manifestly wrong, for an Opera must end happily.

JOHN GAY. Your Objection, Sir, is very just, and is easily remov'd. For you must allow, that in this kind of Drama, 'tis no matter how absurdly things are brought about. So – you Rabble there – run and cry, 'A Reprieve!' Let the Prisoner be brought back to his Wives in Triumph.

Some of the COMPANY *cry, 'A reprieve, a reprieve!'*

PLAYER. All this we must do, to comply with the Taste of the Town.

JOHN GAY. Through the whole Piece you may observe how closely the manners of Gentlemen resemble those of the Gentlemen of the Road. Had the Play remain'd, as I at first intended –

MACNAUGHTON *stands up*.

MACNAUGHTON. This shall not be. I have asked for a moral sort of entertainment. The conclusion of a story is the beginning and end of its morality. If our author does not resemble Our Lord in punishing the bad and rewarding the deserving, then there is no place for stories in a just society. We will have the execution.

Some of the COMPANY *cry, 'No reprieve, no reprieve!' 'He must face the drop', etc.* WILLIAM *removes his* JOHN GAY *costume*.

WILLIAM. Sir, beg to report, we do not have the correct props. We lack a gallows.

MACNAUGHTON. This will not do. We cannot allow the imagination to be subordinate to carpentry. A noose, ho!

A noose is lowered through a grating. Everyone stares at it.

WILLIAM. Captain, this will not serve. There is a theatrical trick to simulate a hanging. I have seen it done. But it requires a full gallows, not your plain rope.

MACNAUGHTON. Who spoke of simulation?

MACNAUGHTON *turns to* HARRY.

Mr Morton. You made a real escape in the town of Rio. And I made a simulation of clemency in order that you might finish your play. Now you offer us a simulation of punishment. But I say the time has come, as we end our voyage, for all debts to be paid. And what fitter ending for a play of convicts than to watch the villain dangle from a rope?

Two SAILORS *come forward. One pulls* HARRY's *hands behind his back. The other places the noose around his neck.* HARRY *prepares himself for the inevitable.*

HARRY. I am not a bad man. I have sought only to cheer others. I made two bad mistakes, a crime and an escape. I should not have made them and I blame only myself. I thank all my fellow players. You gave a good account of yourselves and no more can be said.

Just in the nick of time, there is a cry from the rigging:

SAILOR (*off*). Land ahoy! Land ahoy!

Everyone stops. The quickest thinker is BETT.

BETT. Praise be to the Lord. Our voyage is ended. We have reached Australia! One and all, on your knees and give thanks.

She places her body between HARRY *and* MAC-NAUGHTON. *The* SAILORS *in the execution party sink to their knees.*

SAILOR (*off*) Captain! Captain, it's land. It's land all right.

MACNAUGHTON *looks towards the sound of the lookouts. In that split second,* HARRY *has the rope from off his neck and makes a run for the side. A comic chase where the play, the execution and the arrival in Australia all come together.* HARRY *just avoids his captors. In the split second before he jumps over the side, there is a freeze.*

HARRY. Oh, Neptune, if you have ever loved an actor, love this one now!

Action resumes. HARRY's *in the sea and swimming.*

MACNAUGHTON. Muskets! Muskets and be damned. A gold sovereign for the man that wings him!

SAILORS *bring muskets and fire into the sea.*

EDDIE. Oh, the disparity of forces! A lone man struggling against all that the sea and the invention of gunpowder can hurl at him! A Johnny Thesp swims the last mile to Australia while the Lord God and King George do their level best to bring him down. It's even money King George, six to four King Neptune, and twenty to one King Harry!

The muskets fire again.

MACNAUGHTON. Is there not a man jack of you that can shoot straight?

SAILOR. It's the sway of the boat, Captain!

MACNAUGHTON. He's getting away! He's getting away!

SAILOR. Out of range, Captain!

MACNAUGHTON. The sea will claim him now!

BETT. Can't see him, can't see him!

WILLIAM. He's gone.

MACNAUGHTON *turns to the other* PRISONERS.

MACNAUGHTON. He's gone. Well. Our long voyage is at an end. Gaze upon that shore, for it will circumscribe the remainder of your miserable lives. Abandon all dreams of escape. Gaze upon it and begin your repentance.

The PRISONERS, *stretched out in a line along the side of the boat, contemplate Australia. The tableau is held for a long time. Eventually:*

TOM. I like the look of it. It might be lucky.

They all look at the shore again with TOM's *comment in mind. They all start laughing. They don't know why except that it looks lucky to them too. Then* BETT *points.*

BETT. See there. On that crest.

BEN. Must have caught a bit of driftwood.

GRACE. The bastard. The lucky bastard.

MACNAUGHTON. It will not avail him. He can't live outside the settlement. You will see him in the cells in a few days' time.

Scene Seventeen

On the shore of Australia, HARRY *stands, dripping.*

HARRY. I am left with a Choice. That way lies Civilisation,
that way lies the wildness. They say there are men who can
live as rangers. But am I one such? If I go towards civilisation, will I not, a two-time escaper, face the lash and the
gallows? Even so, there lie my own people, there lies a kind
of England. (*He starts to walk towards the colony.*) But did I
ever love it? How has England ever loved me? That way
Australia. Harry, you are no more. From now it is not enough
to play the hero. You must be the hero. MacHeath lives.

He walks into the bush.

SONG – *to the tune of traditional Australian folk song 'The
Wild Colonial Boy'.*

ALL.
    There was a wild colonial boy
    Who took the name MacHeath
    He jumped the ship in Rio
    And quickly came to grief
    They tried to hang his carcass from
    The yardarm's lofty height
    But he went off a-bushranging
    By morning and by night.

    The tales of his bold exploits
    Are told in verse and song
    He lived among the bolters
    And cared not for right or wrong
    And brave MacHeath has shown us
    And all who've naught to lose
    That if he has the courage
    A beggar yet can choose.

    And from the hour his feet touched shore
    Until this very day
    When children stay up late at night
    At home in Double Bay

Their parents will affright them
With this mythic creature dread:
'Sleep now or bold MacHeath will come
To haunt you in your bed.'

So come away, me hearties
We'll roam the mountains wide
Together we will plunder
Together we will die
We'll wander over valleys
And gallop over plains
For we scorn to live in slavery
Bound down with iron chains.

The End.

A Nick Hern Book

The Convict's Opera first published in Great Britain as a paperback original in 2008 by Nick Hern Books Limited, 14 Larden Road, London W3 7ST, in association with Out of Joint

The Convict's Opera copyright © 2008 Stephen Jeffreys

Stephen Jeffreys has asserted his right to be identified as the author of this work

Cover image designed by Jon Bradfield
(www.jaybeegraphicdesign.co.uk) from photos by John Haynes

Cover designed by Ned Hoste, 2H

Typeset by Nick Hern Books, London
Printed and bound in Great Britain by CPI Bookmarque, Croydon, Surrey

A CIP catalogue record for this book is available from the British Library

ISBN   978 1 84842 015 1